Attitudes Through Idioms

SECOND EDITION

Thomas W. Adams
University of Pennsylvania

Susan R. Kuder
Boston, Massachusetts

Heinle & Heinle Publishers
A Division of Wadsworth, Inc.
Boston, Massachusetts 02116 U.S.A.

The publication of *Attitudes Through Idioms, Second Edition,* was directed by the members of the Newbury House Publishing Team at Heinle & Heinle:

David C. Lee, Editorial Director
Susan Mraz, Marketing Director
Gabrielle B. McDonald, Production Editor

Also participating in the publication of this program were:

Publisher: Stanley J. Galek
Editorial Production Manager: Elizabeth Holthaus
Project Manager: Ros Herion Freese
Associate Editor: Kenneth Mattsson
Associate Marketing Manager: Donna Hamilton
Production Assistant: Maryellen Eschmann
Manufacturing Coordinator: Mary Beth Lynch
Illustrator: Theresa Troise Heidel
Interior Design: Ros Herion Freese
Composition: A+ Publishing Services
Cover Design: Robert Freese

Heinle & Heinle Publishers is a division of Wadsworth, Inc.

Manufactured in the United States of America

Library of Congress Cataloging in Publication Data

Adams, Thomas W., (date)
    Attitudes through idioms / Thomas W. Adams, Susan R. Kuder. - - 2nd
ed.
      p.   cm.
    ISBN 0-8384-3975-6
    1. English language--Textbooks for foreign speakers. 2. English
language–Idioms.   I. Kuder, Susan R., (date). II. Title.
PE1128.A299 1993
428.2'4--dc20   93-9042
                           CIP

Acknowledgments
      The first edition of this text benefited greatly from the comments and suggestions of ESL students at Harvard University who used the materials in a course taught by Tom Adams titled "American Culture through Idioms" in the summer of 1980. A special word of thanks is due to Anne Dow and Bill Biddle for their encouragement of the project.
      For helping in the preparation of the second edition, the authors would like to express their gratitude to the following colleagues, students, and friends: Andy Atzert (University of Pennsylvania) for suggesting activity types, to Margaret Van Naerssen (University of Pennsylvania and Immaculata College) and husband Hans, for providing audiotaped language samples; Lyn Buchheit, Eleanor Schwartz, Brian Teaman, Lynn Simon Voss (all of the University of Pennsylvania), and Rosa Schuette (Washington University, St. Louis) for piloting units and commenting on their effectiveness; to Ruth Pierson Adjogah, several anonymous reviewers from Rochester Institute of Technology, University of Minnesota, and Nova University, and to Yuko Akasaki, Hi-Jean Kim, Peter Martin, Daniella Salama, Jill Turetsky, and Pamela Wassmer (all of the Graduate School of Education of the University of Pennsylvania) for reading through parts of the manuscript and making valuable comments on it; to David Scheller for inputting much of the manuscript and for offering many helpful suggestions along the way; to Kristine Billmyer (University of Pennsylvania) for sharing her expertise of variation in language use and for providing administrative support for the project; and to Ros Freese for her careful editing and creative design ideas.

ISBN: 0-8384-3975-6

10 9 8 7 6 5

Contents

Notes to the Instructor

Description and Organization

Attitudes Through Idioms, Second Edition, presents over 270 idioms commonly used in the United States and examines 24 cultural attitudes associated with them. Each of the 24 units follows a standard framework consisting of seven sections with activities and tasks that can vary greatly from unit to unit.

In the **Warm-up,** students think about the attitude or about issues and events associated with it, thus activating their background knowledge and setting the stage for the rest of the unit.

The **Situation** consists of a conversation or a reading passage in which two idioms illustrating the target attitude are introduced. Students may read the Situation or listen to a recording of it.

The Situation is followed by a question requiring an **Analysis** of some aspect of the conversation or passage. Students choose one of three possible answers, then turn to the Appendix, where an **Explanation** of each answer can be found.

Students then read the target **Attitude,** which is stated in the form of an opinion or assertion of one or more of the characters in the Situation.

The remaining idioms are contextually introduced in four or five **Expansion** sections. Opportunities for using the idioms are provided through the use of exercises, roleplays, and other individual and interactive activities.

Activities in the final section, **Communication,** help students consolidate their knowledge of the idioms and the attitudes they illustrate.

At the back of the text is the **Appendix,** which contains information pertaining to the Analysis and Explanation section, and the **Glossary,** which alphabetically lists all idioms and their definitions. A separate **Answer Key** is available to instructors.

Suggestions on Use

Units need not be studied sequentially, but such an approach might be considered because latter units introduce more idioms than earlier ones, making these units somewhat heavier in content. Units may be omitted or skipped over and returned to later if desired.

Attitudes Through Idioms, Second Edition, is used most effectively by adults having a high-intermediate to advanced proficiency in English.

Attitudes Through Idioms
SECOND EDITION

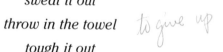

Perseverance 1

call it quits   *give up*

drop a course/class   *hang in there*

bail out (at the first sign of trouble)

keep at it (until one gets it right)

stick with it (to the bitter end)

sweat it out

throw in the towel   to give up

tough it out

stop coming   *given up*   *keep going*

WARM-UP

Write down the names of three people who have become famous because they *persevered*, meaning that they continued doing something in spite of many difficulties, obstacles, or great discouragement. Exchange lists with a classmate and see if you can identify what difficulties these people faced.

Names of people

_____

_____

_____

Difficulties they faced

_____

_____

_____

It is the second week of the semester at college. Tom is at his desk in his dormitory room looking through a course catalog and timetable. Rob, who has a room down the hall, stops by for a visit.

Rob: Isn't it a little late in the game to be choosing classes?

Tom: I'm thinking about **dropping my stats course**.

Rob: Statistics, huh?

Tom: Yeah. We had a quiz this morning and there's no way I could have passed it.

Rob: Not one of my favorite courses.

Tom: What? You took it already?

Rob: Last semester.

Tom: And?

Rob: And what?

Tom: How'd you do?

Rob: Let's just say that my grade was above the arithmetic mean.

Tom: You speak English?

Rob: Above the average, Tom, above the average. Look, I got off to a really rough start, too. How much time did you put in studying for the quiz?

Tom: I had a date last night.

Rob: I don't suppose the two of you spent the evening studying probability or anything like that.

Tom: Not a chance.

Rob: Want some free advice? I say **stick with it**. If you don't let dating get in the way of studying too much, you'll probably do all right in that course.

ANALYSIS & EXPLANATION

Circle the best answer to the question below. Then turn to the appendix, where each answer is explained. If your choice is incorrect, choose again.

Why does Rob advise Tom to continue taking the statistics course?

A. If he could get a good grade in that course, then Tom should be able to, too.
B. He thinks that Tom's reason for quitting isn't very strong.
C. Dating is an activity that Rob doesn't approve of.

ATTITUDE

Rob thinks that if there is a reasonable chance of success, then people should finish what they have started, even in spite of difficulty and obstacles.

EXPANSION A

Put a check mark (✔) if the person continues with something already started.

　　Karen is part of a study group that meets once a week in the library. However, she's been thinking of leaving the group because preparing for it involves a lot more work than she had imagined. After some thought, she decides to **tough it out**. She puts on her coat, gathers her books, and goes to the library.

_____ 1. Sue was in the lead for the first half of the race, but then she tripped over a loose shoestring. When she saw all the other runners pass her, she wanted to **give up**. Instead, she got up and starting running again.

_____ 2. John has been trying to fix his television set for a couple of hours now. He has no idea what is wrong with it, and he is ready to **throw in the towel** and call in a professional. He picks up the phone directory.

_____ 3. Margaret is at a party where she doesn't know anyone, and all the people she has met are boring. She wants to leave, but she doesn't want to offend the host, so she decides to **sweat it out**. She sits down and starts talking to the person next to her.

_____ 4. Fred signed up for four years in the army, but he is thinking about leaving after two. He has a nice job waiting for him in the family business. In the end, however, he decides to **hang in there** and not leave because he feels he should honor his contract. He writes a letter to his family to tell them his decision.

5. June was one of the owners of a catering service. For the first couple of years, business was very good. Last year, however, business was off considerably. Rather than wait to see if things improved, June **bailed out at the first sign of trouble**. She sold her share of the business to the other partners.

6. Kareem was elected president of the student council, a job that turned out to be much more demanding than he had expected. For a while, he considered resigning. In the end, though, he knew a lot of people were depending on him and decided not to **call it quits**. He tore up his letter of resignation.

7. Allison went with her husband to a company party. She developed a bad headache about halfway through the evening. She wanted to go home but knew her husband would be disappointed. So, she decided to **stick with it to the bitter end**. She opened her purse to look for some aspirin.

8. Mark overslept again this morning, and he missed his history class for the sixth time. The maximum number of absences for that class is five. Mark thinks maybe he should **drop the course** so he doesn't fail it. He gets dressed and heads toward the registrar's office.

9. Sandy wants to file her own tax returns this year instead of hiring a tax preparer to do them for her. She worked all day and half the night yesterday, but she kept on making mistakes. She has decided to **keep at it until she gets it right** even if she has to stay up all night again tonight. She sharpens her pencil and switches on her calculator.

> *If at first you don't succeed, try, try again.*
> ***Anonymous***

EXPANSION B   Read the following story and cross out any sentences that do not fit.

Sally isn't one to **give up**. Last year, she crossed the finish line in a cross-country race. ~~Once she read half a book and then returned it to the library~~. Another time, she spent a whole day completing a crossword puzzle. She **hangs in there**, no matter what. That's just the kind of person Sally is.

Sally wants to go to graduate school when she finishes college next year, so she registered to take the entrance exams. The test was last Saturday morning. Unfortunately, Sally wasn't feeling well at all that day. She was afraid she would be too sick to complete the exam, but she **stuck with it to the bitter end** even though the exam was four hours long. She immediately got up from her desk, turned in her test booklet and answer sheet, and walked out of the door. She read the next question and answered it. The last thing Sally would do is **throw in the towel**.

After the exam, Sally ran into Carl on campus. In many ways, Carl and Sally are identical. He is the kind of person who **bails out at the first sign of trouble**. For example, he and Sally were in the same algebra class, but Carl **called it quits** after getting a D on the first quiz. Sally got a bad mark on her quiz too, but she **toughed it out**. She **dropped the course** right after class. Sally can remember one evening when she spent hours trying to solve one algebra problem. She just **kept at it until she got it right**. After working on another problem for only fifteen minutes, she tossed her algebra text into the trash and went to bed.

Sally was anxious to get her test results, but she knew she would have to wait several weeks before she would receive them. During that time, she just had to **sweat it out**. There wasn't really anything else she could do. Finally, they came in the mail. Sally couldn't have been more pleased when she saw her results: she scored in the top 5%. Now she was sure she wouldn't be admitted to graduate school.

> *There is no failure except in no longer trying,*
> *There is no defeat except from within.*
> *Anonymous*

EXPANSION C   Complete the following sentences with an appropriate idiom.

Amy started a new job that she finds very difficult. She is tempted to quit, but her boss tells her it is always hard in the beginning and it will get easier as time goes on. Amy has confidence in her boss and decides to _____*stick with it*_____ .

1. Karen entered a dance contest. After two hours her feet hurt so much that she had to
   _____ .

2. Jack failed the first two exams in his geology course. There is no way he can get a passing grade now, so he decides to _____ .

3. Mike took a final exam in history and did not think he did well. He wanted to know right away if he passed or not but the teacher was slow in correcting the exams. Mike just had to _____ .

4. Max spent hours drawing a picture of the person who robbed him. He went through a whole pad of paper before he was able to draw a picture that was an accurate likeness. Mike _____ .

5. Although Greg did not enjoy his summer job as a construction worker, he decided to _____ because the money was good.

6. It is the final minutes of the championship basketball game. The score is 100 to 75. Oliver is on the losing team. With 60 seconds to go, he knows the team cannot score 25 points. Oliver _____ .

> *If you get up one more time than you fall, you will make it through.*
>
>   ***Anonymous***

EXPANSION D

Use idioms from this unit to complete the following activity.

A *walkathon* is a long-distance walking race that is held to raise money for a charity or special cause. Supporters or sponsors agree to donate a fixed amount of money to a specific person for every mile that person walks. You are a reporter for the local newspaper, and your assignment is to cover a very successful walkathon to raise money for AIDS research. You have just finished interviewing several of the people who had entered the walkathon. Some of them **called it quits** early in the race, while others **stuck with it to the bitter end**. You return to your office and file your report.

THROW IN THE TOWEL

COMMUNICATION   Read and discuss the following.

1. Think of a time when you had to choose between **sweating it out** or **calling it quits.** What was it, and why did you do what you did? Do you feel now that your decision was a good one? Why or why not?

2. Think of several obscure facts (ones that aren't known to many people) and make questions of them. Exchange them with a classmate. If the facts really are obscure, then you and your classmates are unlikely to be able to answer them. If your classmate doesn't get the correct answer after a while, you can say:

    Do you **give up** yet?

    If you are unable to answer your classmate's questions and you want to send a signal that he/she should tell you the answer, you can simply say:

    I **give up**.

3. The expression **throw in the towel** has its origin in the sport of boxing. When one boxer is beating another boxer very badly, the losing boxer's manager might throw a towel into the ring to concede defeat. Another way of admitting defeat is to *wave the white flag.* Do you know how this expression came about?

4. When people continue to resist or struggle even though they are sure to lose, we can say that they are *fighting a losing battle.* Sometimes, people *fight losing battles* because they have no choice. Sometimes, however, people *fight losing battles* even though they don't have to. Can you think of examples of both?

5. Choose one of the following sayings or quotations, or choose one that appeared earlier in the unit. Explain its meaning, or think of a situation that illustrates it.

> *Do what you can, with what you have, where you are.*
> **Theodore Roosevelt**

> *When the going gets tough, the tough get going.*
> **Anonymous**

Acts of Kindness 2

save the day   come to the rescue

do someone a favor   offer one's services

bend over backwards for someone

give someone the shirt off one's back

go out of one's way for someone

go to bat for someone

help (someone) out

lend someone a (helping) hand

WARM-UP

A mother was having a little talk with her young son about kindness. She told him that our purpose in life is to help others. He considered this piece of wisdom for some time and then asked, "If that's what *we're* here for, why are the others here?" How would you have answered him?

_____

_____

_____

_____

Read or listen to the following passage.

Emily and Karen are teenagers who shared a hospital room for over a week. During that time, they became friends. Tomorrow they will both be going home.

Emily: It sure will be nice to be home again and sleep in my own bed. I don't think I'll miss anything about this hospital—except you, of course.

give your many opportunity to help you

Karen: Won't you miss Nurse Hallen a little?

Emily: She was the greatest, wasn't she? She **bent over backwards** to make us feel comfortable. I don't know what they pay her, but it can't be enough.

Karen: I was thinking about maybe getting her a little something from the gift shop downstairs.

Emily: Oh, that would be nice. I'll go halves with you if you like.

Karen: Sounds good to me.

Emily: If we get something for her, do you think we should get something for Nurse Clymer, too?

Karen: Why would we want to do that? She didn't have a kind word for anybody.

Emily: You're right. Bad idea.

to try help a lot

Karen: You have to wonder why she ever went into nursing.

Emily: I know. She didn't **go out of her way for us** once. Well then, that settles that: nothing for our dear Nurse Clymer. So, what do you think Nurse Hallen would like?

Karen: I heard her say she loves chocolates.

ANALYSIS & EXPLANATION

Circle the best answer to the question below. Then turn to the appendix, where each answer is explained. If your choice is incorrect, choose again.

Why did Emily and Karen decide to buy a gift for Nurse Hallen?

A. They felt obligated to do something for her because she had done so much for them.
B. They felt sorry for Nurse Hallen because her job doesn't pay her enough money.
C. They wanted to show their appreciation to her for all the nice things she had done for them.

ATTITUDE

Emily and Karen appreciate it when other people are helpful and considerate.

EXPANSION A

Read the passages below and answer each question with *yes* or *no.*

Kyung Ok Kim is a Korean exchange student who has just started studying at a high school in a small town in the midwest of the United States. Most of the American students are very excited about having an exchange student—most, but not all.

yes Sylvia and her family are hosting Kyung Ok. Sylvia **bent over backwards for Kyung Ok** when she moved in. She introduced her to all of her friends, she took her along to the school football games and spent hours explaining the rules to her, and she invited her to go along to parties. Did Kyung Ok meet a lot of people shortly after she arrived?

yes 1. Emilio remembered what it was like to be a new student, so he **went out of his way** to make Kyung Ok feel at ease. He showed her how to get around school, he explained her schedule to her, he went with her through the cafeteria line on the first day, and he even showed her how to borrow books from the library. Was Emilio helpful to Kyung Ok?

no 2. Walter Ng sat beside Kyung Ok in history. The teacher gave the class a difficult homework assignment and only one day to do it. When Kyung Ok asked Walter if he could help her, he refused to **lend a hand**. That's just the way Walter is. Do you suppose Walter has many friends?

yes 3. Kyung Ok had learned to play the piano in Korea, and she was quite good. When she heard that the school chorus needed a pianist to accompany them, she wanted to **offer her services** because she thought this would be a good way to make a lot of friends. The principal, Mr. Schwartz, thought that Kyung Ok should concentrate on her studies, so he was opposed to the idea. The music teacher, Mrs. Gottlieb, **went to bat for her** and convinced Mr. Schwartz to let her join. Do you suppose that Kyung Ok was grateful to Mrs. Gottlieb?

BEND OVER BACKWARDS FOR SOMEONE

yes   4. One day, Walter was driving home from school when his car got a flat tire. He looked in the trunk for a spare, but saw that it was flat, too. As luck would have it, Sylvia and Kyung Ok drove by just then. Sylvia heard about how nasty Walter had been to Kyung Ok, so she didn't want to **come to his rescue**. Kyung Ok felt sorry for Walter and talked Sylvia into **helping him out**. They stopped and **saved the day** for Walter by taking him to the closest service station where he got the spare fixed. Then, they took him back to his car, where Walter thanked Sylvia. Sylvia told him he should thank Kyung Ok, not her. Walter looked surprised that Kyung Ok would **do him a favor**. He also looked guilty. Do you think Walter might have been feeling bad about the way he treated Kyung Ok?

no   5. The next day at school, Walter was a changed person. When he saw Kyung Ok, he told her that if she ever needed any help with her history lessons—or anything else, she should just let him know. Walter probably would have **given her the shirt off his back** if she had asked for it! Do you think Kyung Ok regrets her decision to stop and **help Walter out**?

Mrs. Albertson has lived in the old house on the corner for about as long as anybody around here can remember. It seems like everybody knows her and everybody likes her. She is different from many other people who live in the city. She's the kind of person who would *give everthing to other one* **give you the shirt off her back** if she thought you needed it.

When Barbara Hoekje was about to have her baby and her husband wasn't home, Mrs. Albertson **lent her a hand** by driving her to the hospital. When the neighborhood association needed to raise money, Mrs. Albertson **offered her services** by organizing a bake sale. When Sandy Miller broke her leg and couldn't drive for six weeks, Mrs. Albertson **helped out** by doing the grocery shopping for her. When a burglar tried breaking into Wendy King's house, Mrs. Albertson **saved the day** by calling the police. When Mark Dickens lost his job, she **bent over backwards** to help him find another one. When Andy Russell went on vacation, she **went out of her way** to keep an eye on his house. When anyone needed a babysitter at the last minute, Mrs. Albertson **came to the rescue**.

Over the years, Mrs. Albertson has **done so many favors for** everyone in the neighborhood. Now, it's time for them to *to go to help* **go to bat for Mrs. Albertson**. Her old house has a leaky roof, the paint is peeling off the walls, the _neighbors all come to repair her leaky roof to paint her walls, and the neighborhood association hold a birthday party to celebrate Mrs. Albertson's birthday._

EXPANSION C   Refer to the events in the Situation at the beginning of this unit to complete the following activities. Use idioms from this unit in your answers.

1. Imagine you are Emily. You overhear Nurse Clymer tell the head nurse that Nurse Hallen needs to develop a better *bedside manner,* meaning that she needs a better attitude when dealing with her patients. You can't believe your ears. You go back to your room and write a note to the head nurse commending Nurse Hallen and condemning Nurse Clymer.

2. Imagine you are Emily. You decide to attach a brief note of thanks to the box of chocolates before giving it to Nurse Hallen. What does the note say?

EXPANSION D   Use idioms from this unit to complete the following roleplays.

1. Work with a classmate to complete this roleplay, which takes place just off campus on a public street during daylight hours. One of you is a stranger and the other is a student. Decide which role you will play. Then read only the paragraph that is for your part.

   Stranger: A *hard luck story* or a *sob story* is a detailed story of severe personal hardship or great misfortune that is intended to appeal to the listener's feelings of pity and compassion. Invent a sob story for yourself, and try to convince the student to come to your rescue.

   Student: You are about to hear a *sob story* from a stranger. A *hard luck story* or a *sob story* is a detailed story of severe personal hardship or great misfortune that is intended to appeal to the listener's feelings of pity and compassion. There is no way you are going to help this person, but you don't want to be rude either.

2. Work with another classmate to complete this roleplay, which takes place just outside of class. One of you is Student A and the other is Student B. Decide which role you will play. Then read only the paragraph that is for your part.

   Student A: You **have gone out of your way** to help Student B several times in the past, but you never even got a word of thanks in return. You are very reluctant to **offer your services** again because you feel he/she is taking advantage of you.

   Student B: You are in big trouble. You parked your car in a restricted zone, and a tow truck has taken your car away. You need to borrow about $100 in cash to get your car back, and you also need someone to drive you to the lot where your car is being kept. Student A has always helped you in the past. You know you can depend on him/her for help.

1. In their book *The Adjusted American* (Harper & Row, 1964), sociologists Putney and Putney claim that most Americans think it is better to do something for others than to do something for themselves. What do you think?

2. If you have access to an English-language card shop, go to the section containing thank-you cards. Copy down the messages from several of the cards that you like especially well, and share them with your classmates.

3. Florence Nightingale (1829–1910) was an English nurse who organized a unit of 38 nurses during the Crimean War to care for the sick and wounded. By the end of the war, she had become famous for her tireless efforts in helping others. Choose someone from your culture who has become famous for his/her acts of kindness, and write a paragraph or prepare a speech about that person.

4. Author Ayn Rand asks her readers if they would risk their lives to help someone who is: (a) drowning, (b) trapped in a fire, (c) stepping in front of a moving vehicle, or (d) hanging by his/her fingernails over a cliff? How would you answer? (If you are interested in knowing what Rand's thinking on the subject is, it can be found in a chapter called "The Ethics of Emergencies" of her 1964 book published by Signet, *The Virtue of Selfishness.*)

5. Choose one of the following quotations. Explain its meaning, or think of a situation that illustrates it.

> *I have always depended on the kindness of strangers.*
>
> **Tennessee Williams**

> *It is one of those beautiful compensations of this life that no one can sincerely try to help another without helping himself.*
>
> **Charles Dudley Warner**

Natural **3** Ability

be all thumbs   lose one's touch

have a green thumb   have two left feet

be a natural born something

be a whiz at something

have a knack for something

have a nose for something

have an (good) eye for something

have the golden touch   *very lucky*

WARM-UP

A *talent* is a special ability to do something especially well. Some talents come about as a result of lots of practice. Some talents come about as a result of a special interest. And some talents come about naturally from birth. Ask several of your classmates to tell you what their talents are, and ask them how their talents came about.

_____

_____

_____

_____

Anna Thomas has a job as a receptionist at a large medical center. One of her duties is to greet the patients. Anna is especially suited for this job because she **has a knack for** matching names and faces. Patients who have only met her once are always impressed when they return and find that she recognizes them immediately and she greets them by name.

Ms. Thomas: Good morning, Mr. Purpura. It's good to see you again.
Mr. Purpura: Good morning. It looks like I'm a little early for my nine o'clock appointment.
Ms. Thomas: Well, why don't you make yourself comfortable, and I'll call you in a few minutes.

Mrs. Stevens: Sorry, I'm a bit late for my appointment. I had the devil of a time finding a parking space.
Ms. Thomas: No problem at all, Mrs. Stevens. Dr. Myers is running a little behind schedule, so your timing couldn't be better. Let's put you in Room 3 this morning. That's the first door on your left. Just go right on back, and the doctor will be in shortly.

Mr. Wheatley: Good morning. You're Anna Thomas, aren't you?
Ms. Thomas: Why, yes. I'm sorry. You're...?
Mr. Wheatley: Mike. Mike Wheatley. I'm here to see Dr. Brundage.
Ms. Thomas: Yes, of course. I see you're down for 9:30. Is this your first visit with us, Mr. Wheatley?
Mr. Wheatley: Second.
Ms. Thomas: Oh.
Mr. Wheatley: Is something wrong?
Ms. Thomas: No.... It's just that I never forget a face, and I would swear I've never set eyes on you before. I guess I must be losing my touch. When was your first appointment?
Mr. Wheatley: Early last July.
Ms. Thomas: Ah! That explains it. I took two weeks of vacation then. But how do you know my name?
Mr. Wheatley: Jill Rosa.
Ms. Thomas: You know Jill?
Mr. Wheatley: We work together.

ANALYSIS & EXPLANATION

Circle the best answer to the question below. Then turn to the appendix, where each answer is explained. If your choice is incorrect, choose again.

Why was Ms. Thomas concerned that she didn't recognize Mr. Wheatley?

A. She felt that if she couldn't greet the patients by name, then she wasn't doing her job properly.
B. She was worried that she might be losing her special ability to remember names.
C. She was somewhat embarrassed because he remembered her name.

ATTITUDE

Ms. Thomas values natural abilities or talents because they enable people to do a job or accomplish a task more easily.

EXPANSION A

Read and complete the following passage.

Mike Wheatley and Jill Rosa are business partners who became so successful so quickly that everyone thought they must **have the golden touch**. Several years ago, they opened a nursery that specializes in growing and selling exotic plants. Today that nursery is the biggest in the city.

Jill **is a whiz at** math, so she takes care of the financial end of the business. In addition to keeping all of the accounts, she is the one who deals with the customers. She's especially good at this because she'**s a natural born salesperson**. Jill **has a knack for** talking people into buying things they don't want, don't need, and can't use.

Mike **has a green thumb**, so he's in charge of growing the plants. But he also **has a good eye for** deciding what goes well together, so when he's not in the greenhouse, Mike is in the shop creating beautiful arrangements from fresh flowers.

The second year of operation, Jill and Mike decided they could use someone to work in the shop and help with deliveries. They hired Steven—Jill and Mike's first and only major business mistake. Steven was a very pleasant person and he tried very hard, but he couldn't seem to get anything right. He **was all thumbs** when it came to making floral arrangements. They looked as though they had been through a hurricane. When he went out to make deliveries, he often tripped over curbs, over steps, and even over himself, completely ruining the arrangements. In addition to **being all thumbs**, it seems Steven also **had two left feet**. The one good thing about Steven was his sense of direction. He **had a nose for** finding the right address without even using a city street map.

As word about Steven got around, business began to drop off. At first, Jill and Mike were afraid maybe they were **losing their touch**. Then they figured out what the problem was. They had a little talk with Steven and suggested that maybe he didn't have what it takes to be a success in the floral business. Almost immediately after Steven stopped working for Jill and Mike, _____

_____

_____

_____

_____

_____

Everyone is good at something, however. Even Steven. Today, he _____

_____

_____

_____

_____

_____

In each of the following, there may be a sentence that does not fit. If there is one, find it and cross it out.

Jane **has a green thumb.** ~~Nothing grows in her garden~~. Her tomato plants have the biggest and juiciest tomatoes her neighbors have ever seen. Her peppers look delicious. She has more green beans than she and her family can possibly eat.

HAVE A GREEN THUMB

1. Vinnie **has a good eye for** buying clothes that go well together. He bought a green shirt and a brown pair of pants. He picked out a striped blue and white shirt and a blue sweater. He bought a purple tie to go with a pink and orange checkered shirt.

2. Gene **is all thumbs.** One night at a party, he spilled his drink all over himself. Another night, he carried a tray of eggs home from the store without breaking any. Last night, he dropped five plates while doing the dishes.

3. Ken **has the golden touch.** He made a million dollars in real estate and then doubled it overnight in the stock market. He will always have to worry about money. Everything he does makes him richer.

4. Sam **has two left feet.** Everyone wants to dance with him. If he isn't bumping into the person next to him, then he's falling down or stepping on his dance partner's foot. It's unlikely that Sam will ever have to worry about too many people asking him to dance with them.

5. Sue **has a knack for** being in the wrong place at the wrong time. Two years ago, she was on an airplane that was hijacked. Last year, she was in a bank during a robbery. Not too long ago, she was in a restaurant at a table next to her favorite film star. And last week, she was stuck in an elevator for three hours.

6. Sandy **is a natural born athlete.** She loves to go horseback riding. She's a champion swimmer. Her diving is great. She's terrific at cross-country running. She's unbeaten at high jumping. She's super on the tennis courts. She's a formidable hockey player. She's not bad at basketball, either.)

7. Phil likes to fish and he **has a nose for** knowing where the best fishing spots are. He is never wrong. His family had fish for dinner every night last week. (Phil never catches anything.)

8. Bill used to be really good at typing. However, he hasn't used a typewriter for years and he thinks he's **lost his touch.** His speed is even better than what it used to be. (He makes more mistakes now than before.)

9. Elaine **is a whiz at** home repairs. She replaced the tile on her kitchen floor. She fixed a friend's leaking pipe in ten minutes. (She threw out her broken coffee maker and bought a new one.) She filled a crack in the sidewalk in front of her house.

EXPANSION C

Write seven statements in which you describe something that you have a talent for or something that you have no talent for. Four or more of the statements must be true, but two or three can be false. When you finish writing your statements, tell them to your classmates and see if they can guess which of your statements are false.

1. **I am a natural born** _____ .

2. **I am a whiz at** _____ .

3. **I am all thumbs** when it comes to _____ .

4. **I have a knack for** _____ .

5. **I have a good eye for** _____ .

6. **I have two left feet** when it comes to _____ .

7. **I have a nose for** _____ .

EXPANSION D

Work with a classmate to complete the following roleplay. One of you is a *talent scout* (a person who travels in search of talented people, often for the fields of acting, sports, or business). One of you is the person whose talents have just been noticed. Decide which role you will play. Then read only the paragraph that describes your role.

Talent Scout: You have searched everywhere for someone to fill the starring role in a film that is scheduled to start shooting in two weeks. You've finally found the right person, and you're not about to take *no* for an answer. Besides, you will get a lot of money if you are able to convince your "find" to sign a contract with you.

Talent Find: You are flattered that a talent scout is interested in you, but you have two reservations. The first is that you really don't think your acting is as good as the scout says. Second, you really don't like or trust this particular talent scout. You are extremely reluctant to enter into any business arrangement at this time.

COMMUNICATION Read and discuss the following.

1. Add to the following list of jobs which someone **having two left feet** probably should not apply for.

   salesperson in an antique shop

   dance teacher

   tight-rope artist

   ski instructor

   _____

   _____

   _____

   _____

2. One way of complimenting a talented person is to say, "You make it look so easy." Under what circumstances might it be appropriate to say this?

3. Skill in the use of the hands is essential for certain jobs. What jobs would someone who **is all thumbs** be disqualified for?

4. Think of a public figure who seems to **have the golden touch**. Why did you choose that person?

5. Explain the meaning of the following quotation, or think of a situation that illustrates it.

> *Anything you're good at contributes to happiness.*
>
> *Bertrand Russell*

Hard Work

goof off   hit the books

work like a dog   fall down on the job

burn the midnight oil

do back-breaking work

keep one's nose to the grindstone

work one's fingers to the bone

WARM-UP

Suppose that you are an employer and you are considering hiring someone. You want to use the following list as a guideline, but you know that some of the categories are more important than others. Number the list in order of importance. Compare your results with those of your classmates. Be prepared to justify your answers. You may add to the list on the lines provided if you like.

relevant experience	ability	dedication to work
age	friendliness	education and training
physical appearance	ethnic or racial background	_____
sex	marital status	_____

Mr. Bello is the vice president of a company that manufactures parts for computers. Today he is in the office talking with Mr. Shuman, a departmental supervisor. Shuman has worked for the company since 1965, the year the company was formed. He began as an engineer in Research & Development, where he put in many long hours of hard work. Shuman soon developed a reputation among his co-workers as someone who **works like a dog.** He eventually was promoted to his present position of departmental supervisor. He will turn 65 this year and he has informed Bello that he plans to retire on his birthday.

Mr. Bello regrets that the company will soon lose one of its most valued employees. He is worried about finding a replacement for Shuman, and so he asks Shuman if he can recommend anyone. Shuman suggests Ms. Fagan. He points out that Fagan works efficiently, that she is productive, and that he has never seen her **fall down on the job.** Bello has also heard of Ms. Fagan's good work and agrees to interview her for the position.

> *Nothing worthwhile comes easily. Half effort does not produce half results. It produces no results. Work—continuous work and hard work—is the only way to accomplish results that last.*
>
> *Hamilton Holt*

Circle the best answer to the question below. Then turn to the appendix, where each answer is explained. If your choice is incorrect, choose again.

Why did Mr. Shuman suggest Ms. Fagan for the position of departmental supervisor?

A. Shuman knows that Fagan is Bello's first choice for his replacement.

B. Fagan does her job extremely well and with great care and energy.

C. He knows that Bello prefers to promote hard workers from within the company rather than hire someone from outside.

ATTITUDE

Both Mr. Bello and Mr. Shuman respect hard work. They value the qualities of diligence, effort, and endurance at the workplace.

EXPANSION A

Carl and Eric are brothers who both have jobs and go to school at night. Carl is a hard worker, but Eric is not. If the sentence below describes Carl, write *C* beside it. If it describes Eric, write *E*.

C   He **works his fingers to the bone**! For example, every day last week he went to the office early, came home late, and brought work home with him.

C   1. He **burns the midnight oil**. He often stays up late at night doing his homework and studying for his exams.

E   2. He **falls down on the job** a lot. He rarely finishes his work. In fact, he sometimes doesn't even get started.

C   3. He **hits the books**. He is a student who reads his assignments very carefully. He prepares himself well for class.

E   4. He **goofs off** a lot. He wastes time at work. Instead of working, he chats with his co-workers. He takes long lunches and a lot of breaks.

C   5. Last summer, he **did back-breaking work**. His job required him to do work that was physically exhausting.

C   6. He **keeps his nose to the grindstone**. He works all the time, even when the work is tiring or boring.

C   7. He **works like a dog**. He works ceaselessly and energetically at his job.

EXPANSION B Choose the best explanation—a, b, or c—for each of the following idioms.

_b_ Stan **works his fingers to the bone**.
a. He only uses his hands in his work.
b. He works hard and seriously.
c. He works until he is tired.

_c_ 1. Sandy **burned the midnight oil** last night.
a. She stayed up because she was afraid of the dark.
b. She was saving electricity.
c. She was up late because she had an exam the next day.

_c_ 2. John **does back-breaking work**.
a. He has huge doctor bills.
b. He works in an office behind a desk.
c. He loads heavy boxes onto trucks all day.

_a_ 3. Sharon often **falls down on the job**.
a. She does not do what is expected of her.
b. She has to stand up a lot on her job.
c. She has accidents on the job.

_b_ 4. Mark **keeps his nose to the grindstone**.
a. He takes three-day weekends.
b. He never stops working.
c. He does not work much.

_c_ 5. Steve **works like a dog**.
a. He works with animals.
b. He works when he wants.
c. He works hard.

_a_ 6. Cathy often **goofs off** at work.
a. She rarely works seriously.
b. She often works seriously.
c. She is a good worker.

_b_ 7. John **hit the books** when he was a student.
a. He got angry when he had to study.
b. He studied a lot.
c. He seldom did his assignments.

> *By working faithfully eight hours a day, you may eventually get to be a boss and work twelve hours a day.*
>
> *Robert Frost*

EXPANSION C

Write a sentence in which you use an idiom from this unit in each of the following situations.

Bill peeled 150 potatoes last night. When he finished, he said he never wanted to see a potato again in his life.

Bill *worked his fingers to the bone* .

1. Steve's boss isn't happy about Steve's performance. The problem isn't that Steve wastes time at work. The problem is that Steve makes a lot of mistakes.

   Steve _____ .

2. Mark's job is that of a *mover*, which means that he packs and transports people's furnishings from one location to another. Last week he had to move a grand piano into an apartment on the seventh floor.

   Mark _____ .

3. Jan stayed up half the night to finish writing a research paper for her history class.

   Jan _____ .

4. Barb is in her room reading a chapter from her biology text. This was the homework assignment her professor gave to the class.

   Barb _____ .

5. Joanne isn't getting much done at work today. She was chatting with her fellow workers this morning. Now she is on the telephone talking to one of her friends.

   Joanne _____ .

6. Jim always arrives at work at 7:00 in the morning and doesn't get home until after 8:00 in the evening. He is busy all day long and rarely takes a break. Sometimes he doesn't even eat lunch.

   Jim _____ .

7. Sally is working on a marketing plan that has to be finished by 5:00 P.M. It is now noon and she was looking forward to having lunch with a fellow worker. She knows, however, that she won't finish the plan in time if she goes to lunch, so she cancels her lunch date.

   Sally _____ .

> *Nothing is really work unless you would rather be doing something else.*
>
> *J. M. Barrie*

EXPANSION D Use idioms from this unit to complete the following activities.

1. You are a student who has always received good grades. This semester, however, your grades have slipped considerably although you have never studied harder. You know your parents will be disappointed and maybe even angry. Write them a letter that assures them you have been **hitting the books**.

2. Imagine that you are Mr. Bello, the character from the situation at the beginning of this unit. Ms. Fagan has applied for a job with the Tell Computer Company, a competitor. A manager at Tell Computer phones you to ask about Fagan's qualifications. What do you say?

3. One of your fellow workers always **goofs off**. As a result, you end up doing the work of two people. You decide to do something about this situation. You might speak to the co-worker or to the boss. Which do you do and what do you say?

COMMUNICATION Read and discuss the following.

1. People who **work their fingers to the bone** are sometimes accused of not taking time to enjoy life. How can too much work be harmful to the well-being of a person?

2. To show their appreciation for a job well done, employers often give their workers promotions. The Peter Principle states that these employees eventually reach their *level of incompetence*, which means that they are promoted to positions for which they do not qualify. What can employers do to avoid this phenomenon from happening?

3. In the United States people who **do back-breaking work**, such as construction workers, often receive larger paychecks than people whose jobs do not require physical labor, such as bank tellers. Why do you think this is so? Is it the case in your country?

4. *Busywork* is work that people do either to keep themselves busy or to give others the appearance that they are actively engaged in work. People might engage in busywork to avoid boredom or they might engage in busywork so others do not think they are lazy. An example of someone doing busywork is a secretary who is tidying his/her desk because all the work has been completed. Give several examples of busywork that you have done.

5. Choose one of the following quotations, or choose one that appeared earlier in the unit. Explain its meaning, or think of a situation that illustrates it.

> *Most people like hard work, especially when they are paying for it.*
> **Franklin B. Jones**

> *I like work; it fascinates me. I can sit and look at it for hours.*
> **Jerome K. Jerome**

Compromise 5

go halfway   *give-and-take*

middle-of-the-road   *not give an inch*

be all or nothing

find middle ground

get/have one's own way

meet someone halfway

stick to one's guns

strike a happy medium

WARM-UP

A *compromise* is an agreement that is reached when one or more people modify their demands. A compromise often is desirable in business transactions or in political positions. In ethical issues, however, a compromise can be seen as dishonorable or shameful. Think of a situation where a compromise would be acceptable and one where it would not.

_____

_____

_____

_____

 **SITUATION** Read or listen to the following passage.

It is seven o'clock in the evening in the Scheller home. Mrs. Scheller is upstairs while her two children, Tom and Dave, are downstairs.

Tom: Mom!
Mother: What is it?
Tom: Mom!
Mother: I'm coming. *(pause)* All right. What's the matter?
Dave: I was watching my favorite program and Dave came in and switched the channel.
Mother: Well, what do you have to say for yourself, young man?
Dave: He never lets me watch what I want to.
Mother: Just answer my question. Did you turn the channel?
Dave: Yes, mother.
Mother: Boys, we've only got one TV set, so you two are simply going to have **go halfway** with each other. Now, let's work out something that both of you can agree to.
Tom: OK. How's this? I'll choose the shows until ten and then Dave can choose after that.
Dave: It's a trick. You know I have to go to bed at ten.
Mother: Tom, I'd like to see some more **give-and-take** on your part.
Tom: Oh, all right. My program is over at eight. If I can finish watching it, then you can choose.
Mother: Is that OK with you, Dave?
Dave: I guess.
Mother: *(smiling)* Now, that's what I like to see. I'll be upstairs. I don't want to hear about this again.

ANALYSIS & EXPLANATION

Circle the best answer to the question below. Then turn to the appendix, where each answer is explained. If your choice is incorrect, choose again.

Why did Mrs. Scheller seem happy at the end?

A. In a short while, it will be the children's bedtime, and she will be able to get some peace and quiet.

B. She will be able to continue doing what she was doing upstairs without any more interruptions from the boys.

C. The boys were able to settle their argument by agreeing to share the television set.

ATTITUDE

Mrs. Scheller feels that differences between people should be settled by compromise.

EXPANSION A

Answer the question at the end of each situation with *yes* or *no.*

___yes___ Lynn is willing to **go halfway.** She feels that if people do not give a little on their position, nothing will ever get done. She does not think people should be so stubborn that they refuse to change their minds. Does Lynn compromise?

_____ 1. Susie always tries to **find middle ground** in an argument. She does not like extremes. She is comfortable when she is halfway between the two sides of a discussion. Does Susie compromise?

_____ 2. With Mike it **is all or nothing.** If he cannot have everything he wants exactly the way he wants it, he would rather not have it at all. Does Mike compromise?

_____ 3. Maria likes to **meet people halfway.** She feels it is important to make decisions that everybody can accept. She will give up part of what she wants for the sake of reaching an agreement. Does Maria compromise?

_____ 4. Ellen **sticks to her guns.** She will not be influenced by people who say she is wrong. No matter how much others try to get her to see their point of view, once she has formed an opinion, she holds on to it. Does Ellen compromise?

STICK TO ONE'S GUNS

_____ 5. Lee is a **middle-of-the-road** person. He can always see the worth of both sides of an argument. He feels that the best decisions are somewhere between the two opposite points of view. Does Lee compromise?

_____ 6. Henry is for **give-and-take.** He feels that in order to reach an agreement, people have to give up part of what they want. He thinks that if people do that, everyone will benefit. Does Henry compromise?

_____ 7. Jim always tries to **strike a happy medium**. He thinks it is important for people to agree, even if they must make concessions to each other. Does Jim compromise?

_____ 8. Mary **doesn't give an inch** in a disagreement. Her position at the beginning of an argument is the same at the end of an argument. Does Mary compromise?

_____ 9. Scott always **gets his own way**. He doesn't ever agree to do what others want to do. Everyone always does what he decides. Does Scott compromise?

EXPANSION B

Read the following passage. Then respond to the statements that follow it; write _A_ for Agree or _D_ for Disagree.

Representative Wilson is from a congressional district that is primarily rural and whose voters are very conservative on most issues. Representative Baker's district comprises people from a major city whose views generally are liberal. A comparison of the voting records of these two representatives shows that they sometimes agree and sometimes disagree on the issues. For example, Wilson opposed but Baker supported a national health plan. They couldn't agree on anything when it came to that issue. However, they worked together to co-sponsor a civil rights bill even though they both had major differences at the beginning. The same was true with a piece of legislation dealing with pollution.

Next came a bill that would provide money for social programs like feeding the homeless. Nothing could convince Wilson to vote for that bill, but Baker supported it enthusiastically. Wilson tried to get Baker's support for a bill that would provide subsidies for farmers, but Baker couldn't be influenced. Baker introduced a bill that extended benefits for the unemployed. Wilson said he could support the bill if Baker made some changes to it, but Baker replied that he would sooner withdraw the bill than modify it. Wilson ended up voting against it, and the bill was defeated. Baker and Wilson worked together to produce a bill that would provide money for education. That was a tough one. At the beginning, there was a wide gap in their positions, but both compromised quite a bit.

The next battle was a bill on crime. Baker wanted most of the money to go for rehabilitation, but Wilson wanted to use the money to build more prisons. The final version of the bill does both. The last bill of the session was about taxes. Both representatives knew they had to raise taxes to pay for all of the bills they had passed earlier, but they were afraid that if they supported a major tax increase, the voters would throw them out of office. So they both voted for a modest tax increase.

___A___   Baker and Wilson **found middle ground** when it came to writing a civil rights bill together.

_____   1. Baker and Wilson **didn't give an inch** when it came to their positions on a national health plan.

_____   2. Wilson showed some **give-and-take** for a bill that would provide meals to homeless people.

_____   3. They were able to **meet each other halfway** when it came to writing an anti-pollution law.

_____   4. Baker and Wilson **struck a happy medium** when it came to voting for a farm subsidy bill.

_____ 5. Baker's position on a benefit package for the unemployed **was all or nothing.**

_____ 6. Wilson **got his own way** when it came to extending benefits to the unemployed.

_____ 7. Baker and Wilson **stuck to their guns** when it came to the education bill.

_____ 8. Baker and Wilson **went halfway** when it came to drafting the crime bill.

_____ 9. When it came to raising taxes, both Wilson and Baker took a **middle-of-the-road** approach.

EXPANSION C

Work in groups to try and find a fair solution to each of the following problems. Your decision may or may not result in a compromise. Use idioms from this unit as you work through the problems together.

1. Debbie Busch needed to replace the heating system in her home. Rob Orsini agreed to install a new one to Debbie Busch's satisfaction. After Orsini completed his work, Busch refused to pay because Orsini installed a model that was more expensive than the one she had chosen.

2. Jim Parker borrowed a car from Sue Fagan. When he returned the car, Fagan was nowhere to be found and Parker had to leave, so he left the car in front of her house. The key was in the ignition. Unfortunately, the car was stolen and was never seen again. Fagan demanded that Parker provide her with a new car.

3. Bill Brundage agreed to cater a dinner party at the home of Steve Grimm. Grimm was entertaining an important business client named Campbell. Brundage was running about two hours late. Campbell left Grimm's house hungry. The next day, Campbell took his business to a competitor. Grimm felt that Brundage was responsible for the lost business, so he refused to pay him for the catered dinner.

4. Mark Tanner rented a car one weekend. Because he was late for a social engagement, Tanner exceeded the speed limit. Suddenly, he spotted an animal crossing the road. He applied the brakes, but they didn't work. An accident ensued in which the car was seriously damaged and the animal was injured. The animal turned out to be Farmer Brown's prize-winning cow, which had escaped earlier that day.

5. A big box of chocolates was delivered to Bonnie Fox one day. Thinking that she must have a secret admirer, she ate them. A week later, she got a bill for the chocolates. She called the store and was surprised when the clerk claimed that she had ordered the chocolates herself! Of course, she knew she had not, and she refused to pay.

1. Work with a classmate to complete this roleplay, which takes place in the office of a company supervisor. One of you is the supervisor and the other is a job applicant who has just been offered a position with the company. Decide which part you will play. Read only the paragraph that describes your role.

   Supervisor: You really hope that this applicant accepts your offer. You have interviewed many people for this position, and this person is by far the best one. However, you are under some pressure from above to stay within your budget. The salary of $35,000 you offered is close to the maximum that you are authorized to make. You can go two thousand dollars a year higher. Anything higher than $37,000 requires approval from your boss.

   Applicant: You have applications in at several companies, and you have reason to believe that you will be offered a position elsewhere, too. You like this company a lot, but you can't consider accepting the salary you were offered. You think you deserve at least three thousand dollars a year more than you were offered. The advertisement for this position stated that the salary was negotiable, so you want to push for the maximum.

2. Work with another classmate to complete this roleplay, which takes place at the check-in counter of an airport. One of you is a traveler and the other is an airline agent. Decide which role you will play. Then read the paragraph that describes your role.

   Traveler: You have an economy ticket for a trip to a city that is five hundred miles away. When you purchased your ticket, you were given your boarding pass, and you were told to show up at the airport thirty minutes before the flight. You did, but now the agent tells you that the flight is overbooked. If you cannot board this flight, you will miss the wedding of a close friend.

   Agent: This flight is overbooked, and you have no more seats in any class. You can offer the following solutions to passengers who will be "bumped." You can book them on a later flight or you can endorse their ticket to another airline. Unfortunately, the passenger who is in front of you now has a ticket that is non-endorsable and non-refundable. You do not have the authority to endorse it to another airline.

Compromise: a deal in which two people get what neither of them wanted.

Anonymous

---

1. Bargaining is a form of compromise. In the United States, the prices of most goods and services are fixed. That is to say, they are not usually open to negotiation. However, a certain amount of bargaining is expected if the purchase involves a car, a house, or even major appliances like washers, dryers, or refrigerators. The prospective buyer makes an offer and the seller makes a counteroffer. This can go back and forth several times. Is this practice similar to what happens in your country? What are the rules of bargaining in your country?

2. Try to remember a time when you **didn't give an inch**. What was it about? Why was it so important to you at the time? Is it just as important to you today?

3. Think of several issues of global importance where various parties disagree. Perhaps the issue is a military conflict, an environmental problem, or an argument about international trade. Briefly outline the areas of disagreement and suggest a way in which the parties to the dispute might **find middle ground**.

4. If you are negotiating something or compromising with someone and you want to indicate that you are making your final offer, you might say, "Take it or leave it." Think of a situation when it would be appropriate to use this expression.

5. Choose the following quotation, or choose the saying on p. 36. Explain its meaning, or think of a situation that illustrates it.

> *This world may be divided into those who take it or leave it and those who split the difference.*
>
> *Ronald Knox*

6 Independence

fend for oneself   *leave the nest*

cut the apron strings   *take care of oneself*

be a big boy/girl now

be (off) on one's own

be old enough to look after oneself

have a mind of one's own

make it on one's own

stand on one's own two feet

吵架

young man or wowan leaves home at the
18 or 17

WARM-UP

Ask the following questions of a classmate. What does it mean to you to be independent? Is an independent person someone who is self-supporting? Someone who makes decisions for himself or herself? What is the earliest age a person in your culture can be considered independent? Is it the same age for both genders?

21. 22

18.

_____

_____

_____

_____

SITUATION

Read or listen to the following passage.

When Steve and Rita Silver got home from work, Steve picked up the letters and packets that had been dropped through the mail slot and landed on the floor of the living room. Most of them were addressed to their son, Greg, who was beginning his senior year in high school. Greg had written to a dozen universities for information on admissions.

Rita: Anything for me?

Steve: Only if you want the bills.

Rita: Thanks, I think I'll pass. Anything else come?

Steve: Just more info on colleges for Greg.

Rita: *(sadly)* Oh.

Steve: Do I detect a note of sadness in your voice, or am I imagining things?

Rita: I guess I've been thinking a lot lately about Greg leaving home in a year.

Steve: Oh, no. These conversations always make me feel old.

Rita: You know, it's almost as if some kind of countdown has begun, and when he leaves, nothing in this family will ever be the same again.

Steve: That's a good way of putting it. I've tried not to think about him **leaving the nest** yet. Maybe we should both just try and make the most of it while he's still here.

Rita: Do you really think he'll be ready to **stand on his own two feet** in another year?

Steve: Do parents ever think their kids are? *(sound of door opening)*

Greg: I'm finished mowing the lawn, and I'm real hungry. What's for dinner?

Rita: *(in a whisper)* One thing's for sure: He isn't going to be ready to cook for himself. *(loudly)* Your favorite: spaghetti!

Greg: Great! Any mail for me today?

Steve: Just the usual.

ANALYSIS & EXPLANATION

Circle the best answer to the question below. Then turn to the appendix, where each answer is explained. If your choice is incorrect, choose again.

Why did Steve say that he has avoided thinking about the day his son will leave home?

A. On that day, Greg's relationship with his parents will change considerably.
B. College will cost the family a lot of money, and there are already many bills to pay.
C. It will mean more work for him because Greg won't be around to do the chores.

ATTITUDE

Steve and Rita expect children to become more independent and self-sufficient from their parents as they reach adulthood.

EXPANSION A

Read the following story and answer the questions at the end.

Later that same evening, the phone rang. Rita picked up the receiver and heard the sound of her mother's voice. After chatting a bit, Rita's mother asked her how Greg was. Rita told her about the conversation she had had earlier with Steve. She asked her mother how she had felt when the time came for Rita to **leave the nest** for the first time. And this is what her mother said:

I'll never forget that summer. You were just nine when you decided you wanted to go to camp for two weeks. I didn't want you to go. In fact, I was dead set against the idea, but you pestered your father and me unmercifully. None of your friends wanted to go, but that didn't influence you one bit. You always did **have a mind of your own.**

I wasn't at all sure you **were old enough to look after yourself**, but I couldn't have been more wrong. Don't you remember how I fussed over you? And you kept saying, "Don't worry, mother, I**'m a big girl now** and I can **take care of myself**." The whole time you **were off on your own** I was worried sick. That's how all parents react, you know, right after their children **cut the apron strings**.

The worst part was the telephone call. You probably don't even remember, do you? Your father and I told you to call us collect if you missed us or if you needed anything—anything at all. You only called us once, at the end of the first week. You were having a ball, and I was miserable. You know what the irony was? You were able to **fend for yourself** just fine, but we discovered that it wasn't as easy for us to **make it on our own**. Maybe we needed you more than you needed us!

Rita and her mother talked for some time about growing up and becoming independent. She thought this talk with her mother did her a lot of good because it made her realize that she began **standing on her own two feet** at a pretty early age. She decided that maybe Greg was at an age where he too could **fend for himself** without any problem.

1. In what ways did Rita show signs of emotional or psychological independence?

   She thought It's almost as if some kind of countdown has begun, and when he leaves nothing in his family will ever be the same again. She said "I'm a big girl now and I can take care of myself.

2. In what ways did she show intellectual independence?

   She only

3. Was Rita financially independent of her parents? What do you base your answer on?

> *There are only two lasting bequests we can hope to give our children. One of these is roots, the other, wings.*
>
> ***Hodding Carter***

EXPANSION B

Answer the question at the end of each situation below with *yes* or *no*.

yes After Jenny turned eleven, she told her parents that she didn't want them to hire a sitter when they went out. She said that there wasn't anything a sitter could do that she couldn't do herself. Does Jenny think she **is old enough to look after herself**?

yes 1. Cindy has just graduated from college and started her first full-time job. The first thing she did was buy a car and rent an apartment. **Is Cindy on her own** now?

yes 2. The kids in the neighborhood where Max lives used to pick fights with him. When that happened, Max's older brother often came to his rescue. When Max turned ten, he told his brother that he didn't need his protection anymore. Was Max trying to **fend for himself**?

_no_ 3. Andy is almost thirty years old, and he has been living at home all his life. Whenever Andy's mother asks him about his plans, he quickly changes the subject. No one really expects Andy to move out. Has Andy **cut the apron strings** yet?

yes 4. Jill's family and friends tried to convince her to go to college instead of looking for a job after high school, but Jill wouldn't let them talk her out of doing what she wanted to. Does Jill **have a mind of her own**?

_no_ 5. Gary commutes to school in a neighboring town. He could live in the dorms at school, but he prefers living at home—at least for the next year or so. Is Gary about to **leave the nest**?

_no_ 6. Mark's apartment is a public health hazard. The sink is always full of dirty dishes, the floors are filthy, and dust is everywhere. Does Mark seem capable of **taking care of himself**?

yes 7. Brian left home when he was eighteen and got a job working in the oil industry. He was able to save most of his paycheck, and after a few years, he quit his job and opened a pizza stand. Today, Brian is the successful owner of a whole chain of pizza parlors! Was Brian able to **make it on his own**?

yes 8. Margo took her young daughter, Ellen, to the Philadelphia International Airport and put her on a plane to Chicago, where she was going to visit her grandmother. At O'Hare Airport in Chicago, a flight attendant told the grandmother that Ellen was a perfect traveler. Was Ellen able to **stand on her own two feet**?

EXPANSION C

In the following passage, Greg's father is rehearsing in his head what he might say to his son. Cross out any sentences that Greg's father is unlikely to say.

Son, I think it's time you and I sat down and had a little talk. You're probably thinking that you're **a big boy now** and you can **stand on your own two feet** so you don't need advice anymore from your old man. Well, you're right. You *are* **old enough to look after yourself**. In fact, you've been **fending for yourself** pretty well for several years now, but do me a favor and listen anyway.

You're seventeen now, and soon you'll be graduating from high school. Before you know it, you'll **be off on your own**. To tell you the truth, I didn't think you would ever **leave the nest** and I'll be glad to see you go. It seems like just yesterday that we brought you home from the hospital. Sometimes it's hard for parents to let go of their children, and sometimes it's hard for kids to **cut the apron strings**, too. I know that you think you can **take care of yourself**, but I want you to know that your mother and I will always be here if you need us. And I'm sure you will because we both know that you'll never **make it on your own**.

EXPANSION D

Refer to the events in the Situation at the beginning of this unit to complete the following activities. Use idioms from this unit in your answers.

1. Suppose you are Greg. You begin to sense that your parents are worried about you **being off on your own** soon. Write down what you would say to convince them that you are perfectly capable of standing on your own two feet.

2. Suppose you are Greg. You are filling out an application for college and see that you have to write a 250-word essay on how **leaving the nest** will change your life. What will you write?

1. A *rite of passage* is an occasion that marks a change of status from one stage of life to another. In the United States, several important rites of passage relate to independence: celebrating one's 16th birthday, getting a driver's license, graduating from high school, being old enough to vote, and celebrating one's 21st birthday. Interview classmates to identify rites of passage in their cultures.

2. When someone does a favor for another, one way of acknowledging the favor or of expressing gratitude is to say:

   > Thanks. I don't know what I'd do without you.   *or*
   > What would I do without you?

   Does this expression suggest that the person cannot **fend for him-** or **herself**? Think of a situation when it would be appropriate to use this expression.

3. Parents often expect their children to follow the rules of the household when they are living at home. Many American teenagers have heard their parents say something like the following when they begin to show too much independence, "While you're living under my roof, you'll do as I say!" or "When you start paying the bills, then you can start making the decisions!" Think of situations that might evoke such responses from a parent.

4. The *empty nest syndrome* is a psychologically depressed state felt by parents after their children have reached adulthood and left home. Do parents in your culture experience such a syndrome?

5. Choose one of the following quotations, or choose one that appeared earlier in the unit. Explain its meaning, or think of a situation that illustrates it.

> *Paddle your own canoe.*
>
> **Edyard Philpots**

> *The young always have the same problem—how to rebel and conform at the same time. They have now solved this by defying their parents and copying one another.*
>
> **Quentin Crisp**

Honesty and Directness

7

be two-faced

be up front

bare one's soul

tell it like it is

get something off one's chest

lay one's cards on the table

look someone in the eye

pull the wool over someone's eyes

speak one's mind

talk behind someone's back

talk out of both sides of one's mouth

WARM-UP

Work with a classmate to try to solve the following problem. The answer is at the end of this unit.

Once upon a time, a clever thief was caught by the king's soldiers. The king, who loved riddles and games, said the following to the thief: "You may make one statement. If you tell the truth, you will be shot. If you lie, you will be hanged." What did the thief say to save himself?

_____

_____

_____

SITUATION

Read or listen to the following passage.

Mr. Lopez supervises a dozen employees at the Ajax Manufacturing Company.   Right now, Lopez and his wife are at home having dinner together. Mrs. Lopez notices that something seems to be bothering her husband.

Mrs. Lopez: Do you want to talk about it?
Mr. Lopez: What?
Mrs. Lopez: Your problem.
Mr. Lopez: Who said I had a problem?
Mrs. Lopez: It's obvious. You haven't touched your food and you've hardly said a word since you got home.
Mr. Lopez: I suppose I can't fool *you* of all people. I do have something on my mind.
Mrs. Lopez: Go on.
Mr. Lopez: Well, you remember John Goodrich, don't you? He started working for us about a year ago and...
Mrs. Lopez: John Goodrich. Oh, yes. I'm sure we met at the company picnic last summer. Two kids? His wife's a computer systems analyst, right?
Mr. Lopez: That's him. So—like I was saying—he's been with the company for about a year. I was sure he liked working for me.
Mrs. Lopez: What changed your mind?
Mr. Lopez: Well, I overheard him **talking behind my back** today. I was passing by his office— he didn't see *me* of course—and he was talking on the phone with someone. I have no idea who it was. Anyway, he was saying what a lousy boss I am. I was shocked. I thought we had a good working relationship.
Mrs. Lopez: That doesn't make sense. At the picnic he went on and on about how much he enjoyed working for you. Are you sure he wasn't talking about someone else?
Mr. Lopez: Not a chance. It was me, all right.
Mrs. Lopez: I had no idea he **was** so **two-faced.**

ANALYSIS & EXPLANATION

Circle the best answer to the question below. Then turn to the appendix, where each answer is explained. If your choice is incorrect, choose again.

Why is Mr. Lopez annoyed with John Goodrich?

A. Lopez innocently discovered that Goodrich thinks he is a bad boss.
B. Employees should not make personal telephone calls during work hours.
C. Lopez had reason to believe that Goodrich thought he was a good boss when, in fact, he thinks the opposite.

ATTITUDE

Mr. and Mrs. Lopez prefer that people be straightforward in their dealings with them. People who are straightforward are honest, direct, and open in their speech and manner.

EXPANSION A

For each of the following situations, put a plus sign (+) if the person's behavior is honest and direct. Put a minus sign (-) if it is not.

___−___ Bill told Steve that he really liked Steve's girlfriend, Gail. The same day, however, he told Jim that he thought Gail was a bore. Bill **is two-faced.**

BE TWO-FACED

_____ 1. Sandy talked to Jill about her most personal problems. Jill now knows just about everything important there is to know about Sandy. Sandy **bared her soul** to Jill.

_____ 2. Mark was allowed to borrow his father's car on the condition that he not take it out of town. Mark drove the car one night to a neighboring town and his father never found out the truth. Mark **pulled the wool over his father's eyes.**

3. Mary did not do her homework because she had forgotten all about it. She thought she might tell her teacher she had lost it, but she decided to tell him what really happened. She **was up front** with her teacher.

4. Barb and Maryanne room together. Maryanne often borrows Barb's clothes without asking her. This bothers Barb, but she has never said anything to Maryanne about it. Finally, she tells Maryanne that she has something she wants to **get off her chest.** She tells her what has been bothering her.

5. Deborah Busch is running for governor. In speeches to the people of her state, she says exactly what she thinks, keeping nothing from them. Debbie Busch **tells it like it is.**

6. When Mary is with Alice, she often criticizes Bill. When she is with Bill, she never criticizes him. Bill has no idea that Mary does this. Mary often **talks behind her friend's back.**

7. During a job interview, Jill made it clear that although she was interested in working for the company, she would have to resign after a year because she would be moving across the country. She thought it was important to **lay her cards on the table.**

8. Joann broke a lamp while playing with her brother. When Joann's mother asked her what happened to the lamp, Joann **looked her in the eye** and told her the truth.

9. At meetings, Betty usually lets everyone else know what her position is on issues. She is someone who **speaks her mind.**

10. When asked if she believed in capital punishment, Senator Benander replied that she believed that criminals should get the punishment they deserve. After the speech, some people thought the Senator was in favor of capital punishment, while others thought she was against. Senator Benander was **talking out of both sides of her mouth.**

> *Being entirely honest with oneself is a good exercise.*
>
> *Sigmund Freud*

EXPANSION B

Choose the best expression(s)—a, b, or c—for each of the following.

_b, c_ By the end of several months of therapy, Sue had revealed to her psychologist most of her deepest secrets and innermost thoughts.
a. Sue **talked behind her therapist's back.**   b. Sue **bared her soul.**
c. Sue **was up front** with her therapist.

_____ 1. Nearly all of the president's advisors are reluctant to criticize his foreign policy. One trusted advisor, however, can always be counted on to say exactly what she thinks.
a. She **speaks her mind.**   b. She **tells it like it is.**
c. She **talks out of both sides of her mouth.**

_____ 2. The small salary increase that Tom got this year really bothers him. Tom thinks his job performance was outstanding, so he made an appointment with his boss to discuss this matter.
a. Tom has something he wants to **get off his chest.**
b. Tom is **pulling the wool over his boss's eyes.**
c. Tom is going to **bare his soul** to his boss.

_____ 3. The residents of Newbury are divided over the issue of how to balance their city budget. Some people want to make businesses pay more in taxes, while others want an increase in property taxes. The mayor's speeches seem to agree with both groups, but nobody knows for sure what she really thinks.
a. The mayor is **speaking out of both sides of her mouth.**
b. The mayor is **laying her cards on the table.**
c. The mayor is **telling it like it is.**

_____ 4. Yesterday, Nancy complimented her officemate, Joanne, on the clothes she was wearing. Later that day, Nancy told someone else that Joanne was dressed like a clown.
a. Nancy **was two-faced.**   b. Nancy **laid all her cards on the table.**
c. Nancy **was talking behind Joanne's back.**

_____ 5. Debbie stayed out late last night. This morning after her alarm clock woke her up, she called her boss and said that she was too sick to work. Debbie's boss believed her.
a. Debbie **got something off her chest.**
b. Debbie **pulled the wool over her boss's eyes.**
c. Debbie **was talking out of both sides of her mouth.**

_____ 6. Don bought a house and then he tore it down to make way for a parking lot. He told the previous owner what his plans were before he bought the property.
a. Don **was two-faced.**   b. Don **got the property off his chest.**
c. Don **laid his cards on the table.**

EXPANSION C

Complete the following sentences with an appropriate idiom from this unit.

Everyone always knows what Sue is thinking and what her position is on issues.

Sue _is up front with everyone_____.

1. Jim was telling stories about Sue, and Sue didn't know anything about it.

   Jim _____.

2. There is something that John has never told anyone before now, and he wants to tell it now.

   John _____.

3. Sally told her mother that she went to a friend's house, but she really went to a party. Her mother never learned the truth.

   Sally _____.

4. Before Mark and Wendy got married, they agreed to tell each other everything about themselves.

   They _____.

5. Joan's boss asked her what she would like to be doing five years from now. Joan told her exactly what her plans were.

   Joan _____.

6. When Andy says something to Dick, Dick generally believes him because of the way Andy acts.

   Andy _____.

7. Bill tries to please people by telling them what he thinks they want to hear. When he talks to Sharon, he tells her one thing, and when he talks to Karen, he tells her something else.

   Bill _____.

8. No one ever can figure out exactly where Mark stands on political issues. Everything he says seems to have several possible meanings or interpretations.

   Mark _____.

9. Sally always says what she's thinking. *(Give two answers.)*

   Sally _____.

   Sally _____.

EXPANSION D   Use idioms from this unit to complete the following activities.

1. Suppose that you are Mr. Lopez, the character in the Situation at the beginning of this unit. You decide that the first thing the following morning, you are going to summon Goodrich to your office for a talk. Make some notes to yourself about what you would like to say to him.

2. Suppose you are Goodrich and that a fellow employee tells you that he saw Lopez passing by your office when you were on the phone. You think there's a good chance Lopez overheard your conversation and you are very worried about it. What will you say to Lopez if he brings up the subject?

3. Suppose that you are the editor of a newspaper in a city that will soon have an election for mayor. Newspaper editors in the United States customarily name the candidates that they support, and they write an editorial column stating the reasons for their choices. Your assignment is to write an editorial about Kevin Folan, one of the candidates. You admire his honesty and integrity.

4. Write a short paragraph in which you mention something that has been bothering you. End your paragraph with the sentence: *I'm glad I got that off my chest* or *I feel so much better now that I got that off my chest.*

COMMUNICATION   Read and discuss the following.

1. Think of situations when students try to **pull the wool over their teachers' eyes.**

2. Does the expression **look someone in the eye** have a similar meaning in your country? If not, what can direct eye contact communicate?

3. Sometimes a person will *stretch the truth* or *stretch a point* in order to support his/her argument or position. For example, a child who wants to stay up later than she normally is permitted to might say to her parents, "But *all* my friends are allowed to stay up late." In fact, only *some* of her friends can. Think of another situation in which you could accuse someone of stretching the truth.

4. Telling the truth to another person might result in offending or hurting the feelings of that person. In order to avoid giving offense or causing hurt, people might instead tell a harmless lie. This practice is known as *telling a little white lie.* An example is telling a sick friend who looks terrible that she looks good or looks better. You hope that your little white lie will cheer your friend up.
    Although telling little white lies runs counter to the attitudes toward honesty and directness in this unit, there are situations when it is acceptable to do so in the United States. Think of other situations where telling little white lies might be appropriate.

5. If people believe that someone is going to make a decision about them based on the information they tell that person, or if people make a mistake and are worried about it being discovered, they might be tempted to *fudge the facts,* which means that they change or exaggerate the facts slightly in order to make themselves look better. Ask a classmate about a situation in which someone they know (or know of) fudged the facts.

6. Politicians and diplomats are often said to be skillful in **talking out of both sides of their mouths.** Think of several controversial issues and how a politician might comment on them. Use the following as an example:

   Question: Are you for or against gun control?
   Answer: People have a right to defend themselves.

7. Choose one of the following quotations, or choose one that appeared earlier in the unit. Explain its meaning, or think of a situation that illustrates it.

> *There is one way to find out if a man is honest—ask him. If he says "yes," you know he is crooked.*
>
> **Groucho Marx**

> *It's better to be quotable than to be honest.*
>
> **Tom Stoppard**

> *Let none of us delude himself by supposing that honesty is always the best policy. It is not.*
>
> **William Inge**

Answer to Warm-up Exercise:

In order to save himself, the thief had to respond with a statement that was neither true nor false. So, he said, "I am going to be hanged."

Fairness 8

play dirty   play fair

be a low blow   get a raw deal

add insult to injury

be a dirty, rotten thing

be a hit below the belt

be an underhanded thing to do

give someone a fair chance

give someone a fair shake

WARM-UP   **Tell a classmate about a time when you (or someone you know) were treated unfairly. Don't tell your classmate what you (or the person you know) did in response. Instead, ask how your classmate would have reacted in the same situation.**

_____

_____

_____

_____

Paul is a senior at Tyree High School. For the past two months he has been dating Amy, the only daughter of very wealthy parents. Paul's best friend, Rich, has heard a rumor about Paul and Amy, and he decides to talk to Paul about it. Here's a part of their conversation:

Rich: Hey, Paul. What's Amy been up to? I haven't seen her around lately.
Paul: Amy who?
Rich: How many Amys do you know?
Paul: Just one.
Rich: Is everything OK between you two?
Paul: Did anyone ever tell you that you ask too many questions?
Rich: All the time. I think you should know there's a rumor going around that you two might be breaking up.
Paul: Word sure travels fast.
Rich: Then it's true?
Paul: Yeah, it's true. We ended it last night.
Rich: That's too bad. Is Amy holding up OK?
Paul: Amy's just fine. She's the one who dumped *me*.
Rich: No.
Paul: You know, just last week we were making plans about getting engaged after graduation. Then yesterday after class she told me she never wanted to see me again.
Rich: That doesn't add up.
Paul: You can say that again. You know what she did then? To **add insult to injury,** she told me the only reason she went out with me was because she liked riding around in my Mustang.
Rich: That's what I call a real **hit below the belt!** *(bell sounds signaling the start of class)*
Paul: Look, I gotta go or I'll be late for class.
Rich: Talk to you later.

ANALYSIS & EXPLANATION

Circle the best answer to the question below. Then turn to the appendix, where each answer is explained. If your choice is incorrect, choose again.

Why was Paul upset with the way Amy ended the relationship?

A. Amy's decision surprised Paul, and the reason she gave for going out with him for so long was unfair.

B. It was unfair of Amy to break up with Paul at school. She should have chosen a more appropriate place to give him the bad news.

C. Amy deceived Paul by not telling him that she had a new boyfriend.

ATTITUDE

Paul and Rich feel that people should be fair to one another. Fairness requires decent and honest treatment, action, or conduct.

EXPANSION A

Read each of the following situations. Then respond to the last statement in each situation; write *A* for Agree or *D* for Disagree.

A Sue tried to get a reservation on a particular flight but was told that it was completely booked. She knew the names of several people who had reserved seats, so she called the airline and canceled their reservations. Then she called again and booked a seat in her name. That **was a dirty, rotten thing to do.** Sue isn't likely to have many friends.

_____ 1. Steve had been waiting for 45 minutes in the checkout line at a supermarket. When he was next to be waited on, the cashier told him that she was closing. All the customers in line behind Steve ran to the next aisle. Steve ended up being last in line again. He **got a raw deal.** Steve will likely return to this supermarket again soon.

_____ 2. George and Doug are equally qualified as mechanical engineers, but George's salary is a lot higher than Doug's, even though they both have worked for the same company for the same number of years. Doug doesn't think that his boss **is giving him a fair shake.** He is more likely than George to look for work elsewhere.

_____ 3. John worked as a salesperson for Apex Corporation. Because his job required him to do a lot of traveling, he had the use of a company car. One day, John's boss called him in and told him that because business had been bad lately, John was out of a job effective immediately. To **add insult to injury,** his boss asked him for the keys to the company car, and John had to take a taxi home that day. John is likely to have fond memories of his days at Apex.

_____ 4. Meg doesn't like Sue at all. One day, she went to the school library and hid the books that she knew Sue would need in order to do a research paper. This **was an underhanded thing to do.** Sue probably did as well as Meg on the research assignment.

_____ 5. Ben and Max were playing baseball last Saturday morning. Ben threw the ball to Max, but Max missed it and the ball went through a neighbor's window. The two started arguing about who was to blame. Ben accused Max of having poor eyesight, slow reflexes, and an ugly wife. He was really **hitting below the belt.** Max is likely to accept blame for breaking the window.

_____ 6. The TransRoad Car Rental Agency advertised a car for only $27 a day. Amy rented one, and when she returned it at the end of the same day, she was given a bill for $79! The bill had lots of hidden charges that she wasn't told about before renting. TransRoad doesn't **play fair.** Amy is likely to recommend this company to her friends.

_____ 7. Nancy was hired because she was the best candidate for the job, not because she and her new boss both went to the same university. A rumor is circulating around the office that she got the job because of who she knows, not because of who she is. The rumor **is a low blow.** Nancy is likely is be upset if she hears about it.

_____ 8. Peg just transferred to a new school where she didn't know anyone. She wanted to try out for the swim team, but the coach told her that the team had already been picked. Peg pleaded for the coach to **give her a fair chance,** but the coach refused. Peg is unlikely to get on the swim team this season.

_____ 9. Mike and Bill had an important business meeting with a potential client at ten o'clock yesterday. Mike didn't want to share the business account with Bill, so he told him that the meeting was for two o'clock. Bill missed the meeting. Mike got the account. He really knows how to **play dirty.** Bill isn't likely to trust Mike in the future.

> _It's not whether you win or lose; it's how you play the game._
>
> _Anonymous_

EXPANSION B

Refer to the events in the Situation at the beginning of this unit and read the passage below. Next, rank order the people in the passage—from those who acted most fairly toward each other to those who acted most unfairly. Discuss your results with your classmates.

Later the same day, Rich saw Amy in the school cafeteria. Rich always liked Amy, but he thought what she did **was** really **a low blow.** Rich tried avoiding her, but Amy was determined to talk to him. She asked him if they could sit together during lunch because she had something on her mind she wanted to tell him. Rich told her he didn't think that was such a good idea, but he changed his mind when Amy pointed out that he wasn't **giving her a fair shake.** He decided he should listen to both sides of the story before making any judgments about Amy, even though he thought Amy's comment about the Mustang **was an underhanded thing to say.**

Amy explained to Rich that she heard Paul didn't love her at all, and that he was only interested in her money. Rich couldn't believe his ears. Whoever said such a thing was really **playing dirty.** Rich knew that Paul didn't care about Amy's money. He also suspected that Joe was behind all of this because he knew that Joe wanted Amy for himself. He also knew that Joe was the kind of person who **would do such a dirty, rotten thing.** Joe doesn't care about what's fair; he only cares about getting what he wants.

Amy admitted to Rich that Joe was the one who told her that Paul didn't love her. Rich told Amy what kind of person he thought Joe was, and he also said that he thought Paul **was getting a raw deal.** He told Amy he thought she hadn't **given Paul a fair chance.** If she wanted to **play fair,** she should tell him what Joe said, and give Paul a chance to convince her that Joe was lying about him.

Most fair: 1. <u>Rich</u>

                2. _____

                3. _____

Least fair: 4. <u>Joe</u>

> *And remember, dearie, never give a sucker an even break.*
>
>   *W. C. Fields*

EXPANSION C

Refer to the events in the Situation at the beginning of this unit to complete the following. Use idioms from this unit in your answers.

1. Imagine that you are Paul. You decide to write a letter to Amy. In the letter, tell her that you think she treated you unfairly; be sure to state why.

2. Imagine that you are Rich. You see Paul shortly after your conversation with Amy. Tell him what Amy told you; then tell him of your suspicions about Joe.

3. Imagine that you are Amy. What do you write in your diary about what happened today?

EXPANSION D

Work with a classmate to complete this roleplay. One of you is the president of a business and the other is the head of a department with five employees. Decide which role you will play. Then read only the paragraph below that describes your role. Use idioms from this unit during your roleplay.

President: One of your department heads has requested a meeting with you. You don't know why. After your department head tells you what he/she wants, you will say that business has been bad lately and that the last person hired must be fired. The department head must inform the employee of this decision. The name of the last person hired is Steve Phillips.

Department Head: You requested a meeting with the president of the company to discuss one of your employees, Steve Phillips. Although Phillips is new to the company, he is by far your best employee. The purpose of your meeting is to recommend a salary increase. You have already told Phillips that you plan to make this recommendation.

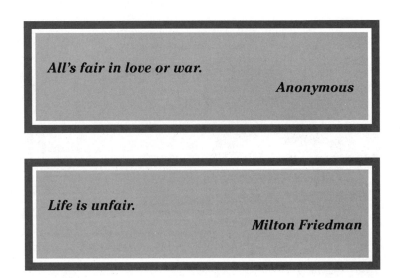

All's fair in love or war.

Anonymous

Life is unfair.

Milton Friedman

COMMUNICATION   Read and complete the following.

1. In the following sentences, some sort of harm has been done to someone. Your job is to make the situation even worse. In other words, **add insult to injury.**

   John laughed at Mary's mistake, and then he _____

   _____

   First, Don pushed Steve to the ground, and then he _____

   _____

   Sharon told Linda that she did not like her dress, and then she _____

   _____

2. You probably have heard sentences that are repetitions of the same sense, for example:

We'll get there when we get there.	Enough is enough.
Whatever happens, happens.	We have to do what we have to do.
It's not over til it's over.	

   The repetition in these sentences ought to be pointless, but each of these sentences is very meaningful. Under what circumstances might you say (or hear) the following:

   What's fair is fair.

3. The Panama Canal was built from 1904–1914 by U.S. military engineers across land leased from the Republic of Panama. In 1978, the U.S. Senate ratified a treaty returning control of the Canal to Panama in the year 2000. In the debate before the treaty was ratified, Senator Hayakawa said that the United States should keep the Canal because "we stole it fair and square." What do you suppose he meant by this remark?

4. An unfair business practice and one that is illegal in many states is called *bait and switch.* The bait is a newspaper ad that gets you to come to a store with the promise of a very cheap price for an item. When you get to the store, the salesperson tells you that the advertised item is no longer available, but a similar item, which costs more, is. The salesperson tries to switch the cheaper item with a more expensive one. Suppose this happened to you. Write a letter of complaint to the store manager, and send a copy to the local Better Business Bureau. Use idioms from this unit in your letter.

5. An unfair attempt to discredit opponents or competitors through malicious or scandalous attacks is known as *mudslinging* (from *mud + sling).* Mudslinging is often associated with political campaigns. Worse than mudslinging are *dirty tricks.* These are unethical or illegal campaign practices or pranks that are intended to damage the campaigns of opposing candidates. Give real or imagined examples of mudslinging and dirty tricks.

6. Choose one of the sayings or quotations that appeared earlier in the unit. Explain its meaning, or think of a situation that illustrates it.

Experience

be green

know the ropes

get one's feet wet

have been around

be a babe in the woods

be an old hand at something

be wet behind the ears

know one's way around

know something like the back of one's hand

not be born yesterday

WARM-UP

A philosophical theory called *experientialism* maintains that we can only know something if we experience it. This theory is commonly expressed in the sentence: There is no substitute for experience. What do you think? Is it possible, for example, to know what pain is or what love is without first experiencing these sensations or emotions?

_____

_____

_____

_____

Meg Harding and Jill Cooper work together in an office. Jill mentioned that she wanted to buy a videotape recorder (VCR), but she didn't know much about them. Meg has offered to help her pick one out. They are shopping for one in an appliance store.

Jill: Oh, look! There must be fifty different kinds of VCRs in this store. Well, where do we begin?

Meg: OK, first I need to know how much you want to spend.

Jill: Oh, I don't know. I guess I can afford up to four hundred dollars. Is that going to be enough?

Meg: No problem. Next, I need to know what features you want.

Jill: But, that's just it. I don't know what I want. Remember I'**m** pretty **green** when it comes to these things.

Meg: Well, for instance, do you want to be able to program your VCR to record a TV show several days in advance?

Jill: Can it do that?

Meg: That and a whole lot more. Just listen....

Jill spends the next few minutes telling Meg all about VCRs, at the end of which time Jill makes her purchase. The two women are in the car on their way home.

Jill: I can't tell you how much I appreciate your help. I'm sure I couldn't have done it without you. Tell me though, how do you know so much about VCRs?

Meg: It's no secret. I used to work in an appliance store. I guess you could say I'**m an old hand at** doing these sorts of things.

ANALYSIS & EXPLANATION

Circle the best answer to the question below. Then turn to the appendix, where each answer is explained. If your choice is incorrect, choose again.

Why did Jill and Meg go shopping together?

A. Neither Jill nor Meg likes to go shopping alone.
B. Jill needed help in choosing a VCR.
C. Meg wanted to take this opportunity to get to know Jill better.

ATTITUDE

Jill values the knowledge or skill that comes from participating directly in an activity rather than from just studying about it.

EXPANSION A

In the following situations, cross out the information that does not fit. Not every situation contains information that needs to be crossed out.

John **is an old hand** at carpentry. He specializes in building cabinets, but he is also very good at making other types of furniture. ~~He hasn't used a hammer in months.~~ Last year, he even made a rocking chair. John has had a lot of experience with carpentry.

1. Mark knows the way to the supermarket **like the back of his hand.** Mark says he could find his way there blindfolded. He often gets lost on his way there. Mark knows the way to the supermarket so well because he works there.

2. Debbie **wasn't born yesterday.** When she goes shopping in a big city, she takes several precautions against theft. For example, she doesn't wear expensive jewelry. She always carries her pocketbook on one side and puts the strap of her pocketbook over her opposite shoulder. She always carries a lot of cash instead of using credit cards. Debbie isn't easily fooled or tricked because she has learned to take precautions when she goes shopping.

3. Ruth **has been around.** She was listening to a lecture about economic conditions in West Africa. The lecturer presented a lot of statistics and then drew some conclusions based on them. Ruth disagreed with the lecturer, saying that she had spent several years in West Africa and she knew the statistics were wrong. Ruth has been to many places and done many things, so it's not easy to fool her.

4. Ricky **is wet behind the ears.** He just joined a large service club, so he doesn't know many of the members yet. ~~He knows all the rules of the club.~~ In fact, he hasn't even received a membership card yet. Ricky is just beginning to familiarize himself with the club.

GET ONE'S FEET WET

5. Dan recently started his first job as a waiter and he is still **getting his feet wet.** On his first day, he spilled soup on a customer's lap. Then he mixed up two orders. He added up the bill correctly. Dan doesn't have much experience at all yet in this job, so he's likely to make mistakes.

6. Bill **is a babe in the woods** when it comes to car maintenance. He put antifreeze/coolant solution into the container that is for the windshield cleaner. He doesn't know how to check the air pressure in his tires. He always checks the oil level. Bill has almost no experience with car maintenance.

7. Lynn **knows the ropes** better than anyone else at work. She knows what to do in just about any circumstance. Last week, she knew the answer to a question that no one—even the boss—knew. If Lynn ever quits her job, she sure will be hard to replace. Lynn knows her job thoroughly because she has a lot of experience in it.

8. Eddie **is** a little bit **green** when it comes to ironing. Last week, he left a hot iron on his favorite shirt for a few minutes and it burned a hole right through it. He sprayed so much starch on another shirt that it felt like cardboard. He puts a perfect crease in his pants every time. Eddie's inexperience with ironing often results in problems.

9. Pat **knows her way around** when it comes to home heating systems. She can tell you the advantages and disadvantages of hot water systems, steam systems, and warm air systems. She can give you an estimate for converting from one system to another. She knows the purchase price of each type. She can even install one! There isn't much that Pat doesn't know about heating systems. She has many years of experience with them.

T   If Ann **is an old hand at** plumbing, she probably knows how to fix a leaky pipe.

F   1. If Kate **wasn't born yesterday** when it comes to playing poker, she probably loses a lot.

F   2. If Ned **is wet behind the ears** when it comes to iceskating, he probably seldom falls down.

T   3. If Sue **knows her way around** her hometown, she probably knows the names of most of the streets.

T   4. If Bill **is green** when it comes to cooking, he probably overcooks or even burns his food a lot.

T   5. If Peter **is a babe in the woods** when it comes to the stockmarket, he probably doesn't pay much attention to the financial pages of the newspaper.

T   6. If Sally **has been around** when it comes to buying insurance policies, she probably knows the names of several insurance companies.

F   7. If Mark **knows the ropes** when it comes to ballroom dancing, he probably steps on his partner's toes a lot.

T   8. If Barb **knows** a particular cave near her home **like the back of her hand,** she probably isn't afraid of getting lost when she goes inside it.

F   9. If Ken just **got his feet wet** recently when it comes to making pottery, he probably turns out professional looking pieces.

> *There is a sucker born every minute.*
> **P. T. Barnum**

> *The only complete catastrophe is the catastrophe from which we learn nothing.*
> **William Ernest Hocking**

EXPANSION C

Complete the following monolog using idioms from this unit. The speaker, Bill, is an experienced mountain climber. He is trying to persuade a friend to come climbing with him. The friend is interested but reluctant because he/she has no experience in this sport.

Look, don't worry. I'**m an old hand** at this. I've been mountain climbing since I was a kid, and I know what I'm doing. I know you'**re wet behind the ears,** but _____

_____

_____

_____

_____

_____

_____

_____

_____

_____

_____

_____

_____

_____

_____

_____

_____

_____

_____

_____

_____

> *Experience without learning is better than learning without experience.*
> **Sigmund Freud**

1. Work with a classmate to complete this roleplay, which is a job interview between a recent college graduate and the hiring agent for a bank that wants to add several people to its credit card division. One of you is the college graduate, and the other is the hiring agent. Decide which role you will play. Then read only the paragraph that describes your role.

   Graduate: You want this job badly, and you have heard that this hiring agent likes to employ people with little or no experience so the company doesn't have to pay them very high salaries. You think that in this instance the fact that you don't **know the ropes** won't hurt your chances at all.

   Agent: You usually have to hire people who **are** a little **wet behind the ears** because your company needs to cut costs by offering low salaries. This time, however, you want to fill this position with someone who has a considerable amount of experience. You are skeptical of the qualifications of the person you are about to interview.

2. Work with another classmate to complete this roleplay between two people who have agreed to paint the exterior of a house. Decide which of you is Painter A and which of you is Painter B. Then read only the paragraph that describes your role.

   Painter A: You have painted lots of houses and you're quite good at it. The only problem is that you are a little bit acrophobic, meaning that you are afraid of heights. The house you are about to paint is four stories high.

   Painter B: You have never painted before, but you are looking forward to the experience. You know your friend has quite a bit of experience in this area, and you are depending on his/her help.

> *The error of youth is to believe that intelligence is a substitute for experience, while the error of age is to believe that experience is a substitute for intelligence.*
>
> *Lyman Bryson*

> *Experience is not what happens to you; it is what you do with what happens to you.*
>
> *Aldous Huxley*

1. Certain activities can only be learned by experiencing them directly. Examples are riding a bicycle, driving a car, or tying shoelaces. What else can only be learned through direct experience? What can be learned by observation?

2. The expression, **know the ropes,** comes from the theater. A stagehand is the person who opens and closes the curtains at the front of a stage as well as the many other curtains in the back, called *backdrops*. The curtains are controlled by pulling various ropes. An experienced stagehand, therefore, is someone who knows which ropes to pull. Use your imagination and try to guess the origins of **be green** and **be wet behind the ears.**

3. Some of the idioms from this unit suggest that there is a direct correlation between age and experience. Which idioms are they? Do you think there is a necessary correlation between the two? Is it possible to be young and relatively experienced or to be old and relatively inexperienced? Support your position with examples.

4. The expression *live and learn* means that the longer we live, the more experiences we have that we can learn from. This expression can be used after we make a mistake or do something we regret. For example, if a friend of yours washes his/her clothes together in very hot water and the colors run, you might say to your friend, "I'll bet you won't do that again. Live and learn!" Think of a time when it would have been appropriate for you to use this expression.

5. Explain the flaw in the reasoning of the job applicant in the following story.

   An employer has just finished interviewing a job applicant. The applicant wants twice the salary that the company normally pays for that position. The employer said, "Well, I'm sure you can do the job, but how can you expect to be paid so much? After all, you have no experience." The applicant replied, "The job is always much harder to do when you don't know anything about it."

6. Choose the following quotation, or choose one that appeared earlier in the unit. Explain its meaning, or think of a situation that illustrates it.

> *Experience is the name everyone gives to his mistakes.*
>
> *Oscar Wilde*

10

Cooperation

pitch in   join forces

be a loner   go it alone

go our/their separate ways

hook up with someone

pool one's resources

put your/our/their heads together

strike off on one's own

team up with someone

WARM-UP

One method for solving specific problems or developing new ideas in groups is known as brainstorming. When people brainstorm, they all come together to contribute their ideas. The emphasis is on getting the ideas out quickly. The group does not discuss or evaluate them until later. One person is selected to write them down.

Brainstorm in the next few minutes about ways that students can save money.

_____

_____

_____

_____

SITUATION
Read or listen to the following passage.

capitalism
socialism
communism
fascism
monopoly

Sue and Ben are history majors who are taking a course called American Economic History. Today's lecture is about to end. Sue and Ben are sitting next to each other.

Prof.: And that about covers it for the rise of the corporate welfare state. Any questions? No? Well, it's just as well because I see we have no time left for questions anyway. The next time we will begin with Chapter Six—The Growth of Monopoly Capitalism. Let me remind you that next Friday is the first test. It covers chapters one through eight, and will count as 25% of your final grade.

Ben: Is it me or is this stuff really tough?

Sue: Don't worry, Ben. I think everybody is having trouble.

Ben: I mean I was OK up to the chapters on technological and organizational innovations, but this stuff is deadly. And that test next week is beginning to scare me.

Sue: You and me both. You wouldn't be interested in **teaming up** to study for it, would you?

Ben: Keep talking. I'm listening.

Sue: Well, we could divide up the workload. I understood the chapters on segmentation in the labor force pretty well.

Ben: And I know the chapters on industrial expansion and urbanization. I think you just got yourself a partner. Let's do it.

Sue: I don't know about you, but I'm feeling a whole lot better about the test since we decided to **join forces.** So when and where do you want to meet?

Ben: How about Sunday?

Sue: That's fine with me.

Ben: The library?

Sue: OK. Meet you in front. How's seven sound?

Ben: Great. See you then.

ANALYSIS & EXPLANATION

Circle the best answer to the question below. Then turn to the appendix, where each answer is explained. If your choice is incorrect, choose again.

Why does Sue suggest that she and Ben study together for the test?

A. She knows that Ben is worried about the test, and without Sue's help, Ben is likely to fail the test.

B. Sue didn't understand the chapters on industrial expansion and urbanization, but Ben did.

C. Sue thinks that both she and Ben are likely to do better on the test if they work together.

ATTITUDE

Sue and Ben believe that cooperation can improve the possibility of success. Cooperation involves a coming together of persons for a shared purpose and for mutual benefit.

EXPANSION A

Write *I* for each sentence that indicates Individual effort. Write *C* for those that indicate Cooperative effort.

__*C*__ If Mary and Paul **join forces,** it means that they work together for a common purpose. They hope that by combining their strengths, the chances of success will be better.

_____ 1. If Sharon is a loner, it means that she generally prefers working by herself rather than working with others to solve problems.

_____ 2. If Don and Dave **hook up,** it means that they come together for a common purpose.

_____ 3. If Raoul wants to **go it alone,** it means that he wants to work by himself.

_____ 4. If Mark and Robert **pool their resources,** it means that they put whatever they have available (including money or belongings) together for a common advantage.

_____ 5. If Kathy's friends **pitch in,** it means that they contribute to a common cause.

_____ 6. If Gene and Ken **put their heads together,** it means that they work together to solve a problem, especially in a joint intellectual effort.

_____ 7. If Lenora **strikes off on her own,** it means that she works apart from anyone else.

_____ 8. If Mary Jane and Tom **team up,** it means that they take some joint action in order to get a particular result.

_____ 9. If Nick and Andy **go their separate ways,** it means that they work apart from each other.

EXPANSION B   Read the passage below and respond with *yes* or *no*.

Mark Benson is a detective who investigates homicides. When he is working on a case, he usually likes to **go it alone.** This time the captain **teamed him up** with a rookie. A *rookie* is someone who has just joined the police department. Benson protested the captain's decision, of course. He reminded her that he **has** always **been a loner,** but the captain was unsympathetic. Then Benson said that a rookie would just get in his way. He asked her to let him **join forces** with someone who had more experience. No luck there either. The captain pointed out that all detectives are expected to **pitch in** and help train rookies.

Later that day, Benson met his new partner, Richard Haddad. They **hooked up** at the scene of the crime. The first thing Benson told Haddad was that he prefers that the two of them **go their separate ways,** but he was making an exception this time because the captain asked him to. Haddad told Benson that they have a lot in common because he, too, likes to **strike off on his own.** When Benson heard that, he decided that the two of them might be able to work together after all. Sure enough, by **pooling their resources,** they solved the case—and in record time. The captain called them in and said, "See what you can accomplish when you **put your heads together**?" The captain was so pleased that she made them permanent partners. That was almost enough to make Benson and Haddad wish their last case had gone unsolved.

yes   Mark Benson probably has investigated many cases in his long career on the police force.

_____ 1. Benson's job probably can be dangerous because he investigates suicides.

_____ 2. The captain probably thought the rookie could learn a lot from Benson.

_____ 3. The captain expected Benson to be cooperative in training the rookie.

_____ 4. Benson saw Haddad for the first time at the scene of the crime.

_____ 5. Haddad and Benson are a lot alike both in terms of experience and temperament.

_____ 6. It was because Haddad and Benson **joined forces** that they solved the crime so quickly.

_____ 7. At the end, the captain decided to let them **go their separate ways.**

> *Many hands make light work.*
> *Anonymous*

EXPANSION C   Use one or more idioms from this unit to answer the question at the end of each of the following situations.

Joe prefers to work by himself. Everyone would be surprised if he agreed to work with others. How would you describe Joe?

He is a loner.

1. John and Roger are best friends. Recently they each got a driver's license, but they have to borrow a car from their parents every time they want to drive somewhere. Neither one has quite enough money to buy a car. Can you suggest a solution?

   _____

2. Sally lives on a block where litter is a big problem. Once every week, she picks up the trash but the job is too big for her to solve alone. What should Sally's neighbors do to help?

   _____

3. Antony is in his dormitory room doing his physics homework. For the last half hour, he has has been working on the same physics problem, and he doesn't think he ever will be able to solve it. Across the hall is a classmate who is experiencing the same frustration. What might they do to solve their problem?

   _____

4. Charles has quite a bit of money that he would like to invest in a business venture, but he has very little practical experience. Rita has a great deal of business experience, but no money in the bank. Both of them are thinking about starting a restaurant. What can they do to improve their chances of success?

   _____

5. Naomi and Ruth bought a printer for their computer, but it has to be unpacked, assembled, and then connected to the computer. They are reading the instruction manual together. How can you describe what they are doing?

   _____

6. Sandy, Barb, and Margaret were in business together for many years. They owned and operated a successful photography shop. One day, Barb called the others together and said she had an important announcement to make. She had decided to open her own business on the other side of town. How can you describe Barb's action?

   _____

EXPANSION D

Using idioms from this unit, comment on the people in the following passage.

On Sunday evening at 7:00 sharp, Ben went to the school library where Sue was waiting for him on the front steps. With her were two other classmates, Dan and Bonnie. Sue told Ben that Dan and Bonnie had heard about their study group and that they would like to join. They also thought the course material was difficult. Ben thought it would be a good idea to let them join because the work would be cut in half if four people rather than two were preparing for the exam. The test covered eight chapters, so each person could take two chapters and present them to the group. Everybody agreed, and they went inside to find a table where they could study.

Unfortunately, Dan wasted a lot of time talking about everything but history. The group wasn't making much progress, so Bonnie decided to study by herself. Finally, Sue told Dan that maybe it wasn't such a good idea for them to be working together after all, so Dan left. In the next couple of hours, Sue and Ben got a lot of work done. The moral of the lesson is that more isn't always better.

Read and discuss the following.

1. *Groupthink* is the name given to the practice of decision-making or policy-making by a group such as a board of directors or a research team. This approach is sometimes thought to result in a lack of individual creativity or personal responsibility. What kinds of problems or issues might be best dealt with by group consensus, and what kinds by individuals acting independently?

2. Some people belong to clubs and associations in order to make business and social contacts or for increased status. Such people are called *joiners*. People who avoid the company of others are called *loners*. This term does not imply that they are unhappy. In fact, most loners are loners by choice. Is it common to find joiners and loners in your country? Which are you? Explain your choice.

3. On many public trash cans across the United States, you will notice the words, "Pitch in." You learned that this idiom means "join in" or "contribute to a common cause," but it has an additional meaning in this context. Can you guess what it is? Can you explain why both definitions are appropriate in the context of trash cans?

4. The following sentence sometimes appears at the end of a business letter or an office memo in which the writer makes a request of the reader(s): "Your cooperation in this matter is appreciated." For example, the boss notices that some employees have been leaving work early, so she sends a memo to remind them that the workday ends at 5:00. The memo ends with, "Your cooperation in this matter is appreciated." What does this sentence really mean? Write a short memo to someone in which you voice a complaint or make a request. Be sure to end your memo with the sentence about cooperation.

buddy - found

5. A *buddy* is a friendly companion. The *buddy system* is a form of cooperation in which two people watch out for each other or become responsible for each other's safety. The buddy system might be used when people engage in activities such as swimming, scuba diving, or mountain climbing. Why do you think the buddy system might be used for these activities? When else might it be used?

6. Choose one of the following sayings or quotations, or choose the one that appeared earlier in the unit. Explain its meaning, or think of a situation that illustrates it.

> *Two heads are better than one.*
> *Anonymous*

> *And so we plow along, as the fly said to the ox.*
> *H. W. Longfellow*

11 Improbability

be a long shot
beat the odds
be the underdog
be out of one's hands
be an uphill battle/struggle
be like looking for a needle in a haystack
cards are stacked against one
hands are/were tied
have a snowball's chance in hell
see the writing on the wall

WARM-UP

The following is the beginning of a list of situations or activities in which people try to win even though their chances may not be very good. Add to the list and then compare your list with your classmates' lists.

Poker

Horse racing

SITUATION

Read or listen to the following passage.

Election day in the United States is held on the first Tuesday in November. On the evening of the last election, Tom Phillips went to the *polls* (the place where people vote) but was told by an official there that he couldn't vote because his registration had been cancelled. According to the law in the state where Tom lived, the names of people who do not vote for more than two years are removed from the voter registration lists. Tom was very upset to learn that he couldn't vote, but there was no point in arguing with the official. After all, there was nothing the official could do—her **hands were tied.** She told Tom that the only way he could vote in this election was if he went to a judge, pleaded his case, and received special permission to vote. Tom thanked her for her suggestion, but he could see that the **cards were stacked against him.** He knew that by the time he did all of this, the polls would be closed and it would be too late to vote. He went home and watched the election returns on television. Later that night, it was announced that the candidate Tom had planned to vote for won the election. That made Tom feel a little bit better.

ANALYSIS & EXPLANATION

Circle the best answer to the question below. Then turn to the appendix, where each answer is explained. If your choice is incorrect, choose again.

Why didn't Tom ask the judge for permission to vote?

A. He could see that there probably wasn't enough time left.
B. He wanted to get back home and watch the results of the election on television.
C. He thought that the candidate he supported would win the election anyway.

ATTITUDE

Tom thinks it is important to recognize when a desired outcome is unlikely or impossible.

EXPANSION A

The following situations deal with what somebody would like to happen. Answer the question at the end of each situation with *yes* or *no*.

_no_   Sam loves to go to parties, so he misses a lot of classes and he fails most of his exams. In other words, he **has a snowball's chance in hell** of passing his courses. Do you think Sam studies much?

_____ 1. Mark would like a promotion, but he knows his name isn't on the list of people being considered. In other words, he **sees the writing on the wall.** Do you think Mark's boss is pleased with Mark's work?

_____ 2. Mike wanted to borrow some money from his sister Sue, but Sue didn't have any to spare. She told him she was sorry, but her **hands were tied.** Do you think Sue would have lent him the money if she had had some?

_No_ 3. Lucy is going to ask her boss for a raise even though she knows that business hasn't been good lately. In other words, she knows her request **is a long shot.** Is it likely that Lucy will get the raise?

_N_ 4. Joan is running for president of the student council. The students have always voted for a senior but Joan is only a sophomore. In other words, the **cards are stacked against her.** Do you think Joan will win the election?

_Y_ 5. Ted went to the race track and bet all of his money on a horse that has never won. Ted just had a feeling that today the horse would come in first. Nearly everyone else bet on other horses. In other words, Ted thought he could **beat the odds.** Do you think Ted's chances of winning were slim?

_N_ 6. Jenny is a bank auditor. She examines and certifies the financial records of banks. When money cannot be accounted for, it's Jenny's job to find out what happened to it. Sometimes, it's easy to do this, but often it's not. In other words, it can **be like looking for a needle in a haystack.** Do you think Jenny's chances of finding missing money are always good?

_N_ 7. Tim would like to see a change in his company's vacation policy, but he knows it is very difficult to change company policy. In other words, it will **be an uphill battle** for him. Do you think Tim's chances of getting the company to change its policy are good?

_N_ 8. Sam is going to play chess with the school champion, Margaret. Margaret hasn't lost a game in years, so most people think she will win against Sam. In other words, most students think Sam **is the underdog** in this contest. Do you think Sam's chances of winning are good?

_N_ 9. Andy bought a pair of pants that were on sale. When he got home, he decided he didn't like them, so he went back to the store. The clerk told him that the store policy was that discounted merchandise could not be returned or exchanged. There was nothing the clerk could do. In other words, it **was out of the clerk's hands.** Do you think Andy's chances of getting a refund were great?

> *The greatest pleasure in life is doing what people say you cannot do.*
>
> *Walter Bagehot*

EXPANSION B

Read each of the following situations. Then respond to the last statement in each situation; write *A* for Agree or *D* for Disagree.

_A_   Sue **has a snowball's chance in hell** of getting a job with a particular company. It seems pointless for her even to fill out an application form.

_d_   1. Bill is flipping through a dictionary to find a word he is trying to remember. This **is like looking for a needle in a haystack.** It is likely that Bill's strategy will work.

_a_   2. Jane didn't get a good look at the man who stole her car. Now, she is looking through photographs of criminals that the police gave her. She hopes to identify the thief from among the photographs, but she knows it **is a long shot.** Jane is probably wasting her time.

_a_   3. Marge wants to be on her school basketball team, but she is very short and her eyesight is bad. The **cards are stacked against her.** Maybe Marge should develop an interest in a different activity.

_a_   4. Peter came from a poor family and grew up in a very bad neighborhood. Many of the kids in the neighborhood were born into poverty and will die in poverty. But not Peter. He **beat the odds** by studying hard in school and getting a good job after graduation.

_a_   5. Jill paid the tuition for a course. On the second day of class, Jill decided she wanted to drop the course and get her money back. She spoke to an administrator who said that his **hands were tied** in this matter. He pointed out that no refunds could be issued after the start of classes. Even if the administrator wanted to help Jill, the policy prevents him from intervening.

_a_   6. All of Ed's officemates got good annual increases in their salaries. Ed didn't get any increase at all. Ed had some doubts about his future with the company before, but now he clearly **sees the writing on the wall.** Maybe Ed should start looking for a job elsewhere.

_a_   7. Felicia works in the post office. A customer who mailed a letter several minutes ago has just returned to say that he doesn't want to send the letter after all. Felicia checks on the letter, but discovers that it has been taken away. She tells the customer that it'**s out of her hands.** The customer should accept that there is nothing Felicia can do to help.

_a_   8. Randy entered a cross-country bicycle race. He was in the lead for most of the race, but then he got a flat tire and lost five minutes making the repairs. Finishing in first place will **be an uphill struggle** now. Randy might still win, but it will be very difficult.

_d_   9. Until last week, Marian's chances of winning the championship tennis match were thought to be very good. But then Marian sprained her ankle. She is still planning to play, but now she'**s the underdog.** Marian is expected to win.

EXPANSION C

Use one idiom from this unit to answer each of the following questions. Several idioms may be acceptable as answers.

What can you say about someone who won a game of chance?

She beat the odds.

1. What can you say to someone who is searching for something that will be very difficult to find?

   looking for needle in a haystack

2. What can you say that describes someone who is seen as the probable loser in a conflict or contest?

   be the underdog

3. What can you say to someone who realizes that a bad situation is inevitable?

   cards are stacked against me, be out of one's hands

4. What can you say to describe a situation in which someone is trying to succeed even though the effort is very tiring and difficult?

   be a long shot

5. What can you say to someone who has virtually no chance of winning or succeeding?

   have a snowball' in hell   cards are stacked against me

6. What can you say to describe someone who is unable to intervene in a situation?

   hands is tied

7. What can you say to describe a situation in which someone is unable to intervene?

   be out of one's hand

8. What can you say to describe a situation in which a desired result is unlikely?

   have a snowball's chance in hell

zwt 弓 bkbb 3 a.n.

> *The improbable happens just often enough to*
> *make life either disturbing or delightful.*
> **William Feather**

1. As she did every morning, Mrs. Smith opened her back door and let Oscar outside one day two weeks ago. Oscar is the name of her cat, and that was the last time she saw him. Oscar would always return home before dark, so Mrs. Smith has become very worried. She put notices up around the neighborhood that described Oscar and offered a reward for information leading to his return.

   _____

   _____

   _____

   _____

   _____

   _____

   _____

   _____

   _____

   _____

   _____

2. Bill Otis just got home from work and discovered that a window in his living room had been broken. Among the pieces of glass on the floor is a baseball. This is the third time this month this has happened. He is angry and decides to call the police.

   _____

   _____

   _____

   _____

   _____

   _____

   _____

   _____

   _____

   _____

   _____

3. About an hour earlier, Jenny had started raking the leaves in her backyard. She was nearly finished. As she stood looking at the big pile of leaves, she put her hand to her ear. She noticed that her earring was missing. She was sure she was wearing the earring when she started raking. Her smile turned into a frown.

_____

_____

_____

_____

_____

_____

_____

_____

_____

_____

4. John had arranged to meet Sue inside the university cafeteria at noon. He was running a little bit late, and it was 12:15 when he reached the entrance to the cafeteria. He hoped Sue wouldn't be angry. To get in the cafeteria, John had to show his school identification card. John reached into his back pocket, but his wallet wasn't there. He remembered that he had left his wallet in his room. He tried explaining the situation, but the guard said that the cafeteria has a firm rule about admittance: no ID card, no entry—no exceptions.

_____

_____

_____

_____

_____

_____

_____

_____

_____

_____

_____

1. One of the idioms in this unit comes from card playing: **cards are stacked against one.** When one player stacks a *deck* (pack) of cards, he/she cheats by arranging the cards in a particular order. The dealer is the person who *shuffles* (mixes) the cards and then *deals* (distributes) them. A *hand* is all the cards dealt to one player. Now that you know many of the key terms associated with card playing, see if you can figure out the meaning of another idiom that has been borrowed from this activity: *The hand is dealt.*

2. *Dice* are small white cubes that are usually used in pairs for games of chance. On each side of the cube is a different number of black dots, from one to six. *Loaded dice* are secretly and unfairly weighted so as to increase the chances of certain combinations to appear face up. When your chances of winning have been decreased unfairly or fraudently, you can say that the *dice were loaded against you* from the very beginning. Think of a situation when this happened to you or to someone you know.

3. A *simile* is a figure of speech in which a similarity between two unlike things or actions is compared. Most similes are introduced by the words "as" or "like." In this unit, you were introduced to the second half of a simile: **like looking for a needle in a haystack.** Think of actions that might be used with this idiom, as in the following example: Trying to find the ring you lost at the beach would **be like looking for a needle in a haystack.**

4. A person who is expected to lose is known as the *underdog.* An underdog is thought to be the probable loser in a contest or conflict because he or she is at a disadvantage. For example, in most political races in the United States when a newcomer challenges a well-known incumbent (the person currently in office), the newcomer usually is seen as the underdog. An underdog can be a person, a group, or a nation. Think of conflicts or contests where there is an underdog. Think of a situation where the underdog won.

5. A well-known concept in the field of statistics is the *gambler's fallacy,* which means that people sometimes don't realize that events which follow each other might be independent of each other. For example, if you lose at cards ten times in a row, you might think that your chances of winning on the eleventh try are better than fifty-fifty. They aren't, however, because each time you play cards, it is an independent event. Can you think of other events that illustrate the gambler's fallacy?

6. Choose one of the quotations that appeared earlier in the unit. Explain its meaning, or think of a situation that illustrates it.

12 Friendliness

put someone at ease   *warm up to someone*

be cool toward someone   *make someone feel at home*

get up on the wrong side of the bed

give someone a hard/rough time

give someone a warm welcome

give someone the cold shoulder

not give someone the time of day

welcome someone with open arms

WARM-UP

What does it mean to be a friendly person? What is a friendly greeting? Friendly advice? A friendly warning?

_____

_____

_____

_____

_____

_____

Nancy and Susan are not only roommates but also best friends. Nancy always gets up earlier than Susan to make breakfast. It's ready now, and she is about to call Susan to the table.

Nancy: Breakfast is ready! Are you up yet?

Susan: I'm coming. I'm coming.

Nancy: Good morning. There's orange juice on the table—freshly squeezed. The coffee's hot, and your eggs'll be ready in a couple of minutes.

Susan: Oh, not eggs again.

Nancy: You don't want eggs? I can make something else, I guess. No trouble. How about some nice pancakes?

Susan: No, never mind. Eggs are fine.

Nancy: Did you hear the weather report? We're supposed to get some rain. We really need it.

Susan: Slippery roads.

Nancy: What'd you say?

Susan: If it rains, there'll be slippery roads—and accidents. Lots of accidents.

Nancy: Right. Are you OK?

Susan: This coffee's cold.

Nancy: Here, let me freshen it up. *(She adds hot coffee to Susan's cup.)* Is that better?

Susan: Now it's too hot. I think I burned my lips.

Nancy: What is the matter with you? You are not yourself today.

Susan: I don't know what you're talking about.

Nancy: Oh, come on! You've been **giving me a hard time** ever since you got up. I can't seem to do anything right this morning.

Susan: I'm sorry. Really, I am. It's nothing personal. I woke up feeling lousy. I guess you could say I **got up on the wrong side of the bed.**

Nancy: I know what you mean. We all have days like that.

ANALYSIS & EXPLANATION

Circle the best answer to the question below. Then turn to the appendix, where each answer is explained. If your choice is incorrect, choose again.

What did Nancy think of Susan's behavior?

A. She thought it was normal because she knows that everyone has bad days.
B. She thought her behavior was rude and unusual because Susan complained about everything.
C. She thought it was strange because Susan usually talks a lot more in the morning.

ATTITUDE

Nancy thinks that social relationships should be characterized by friendly behavior—that is, behavior that is agreeable and pleasant.

EXPANSION A

For each of the following situations, put a plus sign (+) if the behavior is friendly or a minus sign (-) if it is not.

___−___ You are spending the day with one of your friends, John. Usually, he is very pleasant to be with, but today nothing anyone does seems to please him. You don't know why he is acting the way he is. You suppose he **got up on the wrong side of the bed.**

_____ 1. You went to a friend's house for dinner. You hadn't met anyone else in the family before that night. Everyone was very pleasant and very easy to talk to. You felt they **gave you a warm welcome.**

___−___ 2. At a party you run into Steve, a former classmate. You haven't seen much of each other lately, so you ask how he is. He virtually ignores you. He **won't give you the time of day.**

___−___ 3. You are walking down the street and you spot someone you have met socially several times. You wave to him but he doesn't respond. You're sure he saw you, and you don't know why he **gave you the cold shoulder.**

___+___ 4. When you first met Jill, you didn't think the two of you could ever be friendly. After you got to know her better, you discovered that there were many things you liked about her. It took some time, but eventually you **warmed up to her.**

___−___ 5. One of your neighbors, George, introduced a visiting aunt to you. You shook hands and tried to make conversation, but you got the impression that she wasn't interested in talking to you. You can't explain why she **was cool toward you.**

GET UP ON THE WRONG SIDE OF THE BED

_____ 6. You return to visit your elementary school. Much to your surprise, your favorite teacher is still teaching there. She is excited to see you, and she **welcomes you with open arms.**

_____ 7. You were interviewed yesterday for a job that you would really like to have. The person who interviewed you, Randy Ferrer, started by telling you to call him by his first name and then he offered you a cup of coffee. You think you did well in part because Mr. Ferrer helped **put you at ease.**

_____ 8. You were at the checkout counter of a grocery store. While you were in line, you overheard a customer **giving the cashier a rough time** about the careless way he was packing the groceries in bags.

_____ 9. You have been transferred to another office, which you must share with someone who has been there for some time. You felt a little bit uncomfortable on the first day, but your new officemate helped you settle in. When she finished, she said, "If there's anything else I can do, just give a holler." You think you're going to like your new arrangement because she **made you feel right at home.**

> *You cannot use your friends and have them, too.*
>
> *Anonymous*

EXPANSION B

Read the passage below. Then respond to the statements that follow it; write *A* for Agree or *D* for Disagree.

Jan and Marge left their apartment and were on their way to work when they ran into Marge's ex-husband. Their marriage had only lasted three weeks, and they haven't exactly been on friendly terms since Marge filed for a divorce. They seldom see each other because Bob spends a lot of time traveling, but when they do, she always **gives him the cold shoulder.** Today was no exception. Bob saw Marge first and he waved, but Marge just ignored him and kept on walking. This is unusual for Marge because she is one of the friendliest people anyone could ever meet. She always **welcomes everyone with open arms**—everyone except Bob.

From time to time, Jan would see Bob at parties and at first she **was cool toward him.** After a while though, she began to **warm up to him** a little. She thought he seemed like a nice enough guy, but she also knows that people aren't always what they seem to be.

Once Bob came to the apartment to see Marge, but she had gone out for a few minutes. Jan answered the door, and when she saw who it was, she **gave him the same warm welcome** she gives to everyone who visits. Bob wondered if he could wait until Marge got back, so Jan invited him in. She asked him if he wanted a little something to eat or drink. In fact, she did her best to **make him feel at home** and to **put him at ease,** but he seemed to have a lot on his mind. When Marge came back, she was plainly unhappy to see him there. He tried talking to her, but she **would barely give him the time of day**. Bob didn't stay long.

Later that day, Jan asked Marge about her marriage to Bob and the reasons for their divorce. Marge had always avoided the subject before, but today she opened up. It seems that Bob liked being married so much that he had secretly taken several wives at the same time. Marge didn't much like the idea of polygamy, and she certainly didn't like Bob's lies.

_A_   Bob probably lives in the same city as Marge and Jan, but probably not in the same neighborhood.

_____   1. Jan and Bob probably do not have any of the same friends.

_____   2. Jan probably knew Bob before his marriage to Marge.

_____   3. Jan probably spoke at length to Bob when she saw him at parties.

_____   4. Jan probably doesn't know Bob very well.

_____   5. Marge probably had invited Bob to visit her the day that he came when she had stepped out.

_____   6. Bob didn't stay long the day he visited Marge because he probably had other things to do and places to go.

_____   7. When Bob is "traveling," he probably is visiting his other wives.

_____   8. Jan probably will be more careful around Bob if she ever sees him again.

EXPANSION C

Use an idiom from this unit to describe the behavior of the person in each of the following situations. There may be more than one idiom for each situation.

A stranger approached Barb on the street and politely asked her for directions. Barb ignored the question and kept on walking.

Barb wouldn't give the stranger the time of day.

1. Jim had an appointment with a new dentist. He always got very nervous the moment he sat down in the dentist's chair. This dentist, however, had a friendly manner that made Jim feel comfortable.

2. Sue wasn't very friendly toward Pam when Pam and her family moved in next door. But when she discovered that they had many of the same interests, everything changed.

3. Alice quit her last job because she couldn't stand her boss. When she saw him yesterday on the bus, she walked right by him without saying anything.

4. When Mark answered his doorbell, he saw his best friend standing there. They hadn't seen each other for several months.

5. Jay has been complaining all day long. No matter what happens, nothing seems to please him.

6. Bill was sitting in the back of class whispering to another student during a test. His teacher, who was sitting in the front, stood up and looked right at him.

7. Mary was in line behind John in the school cafeteria. She tried to strike up a conversation with him, but he seemed indifferent to her.

8. When Donna started working at her new job, her new officemates offered their assistance and did everything they could to make her feel comfortable.

> *Be courteous to all, but intimate with few, and let those few be well tried before you give them your confidence.*
>
> *George Washington*

EXPANSION D   Using idioms from this unit, finish the following story.

Steve Chun has invited his boss home for dinner. Steve is understandably very nervous about entertaining his boss over dinner, but Steve's wife, Ellen, has assured him that everything will be fine. Steve's boss is a little bit shy when meeting new people, but Ellen is excellent at **putting people at ease.**

When Steve's boss arrives, Ellen has the vague impression that they've met before but she can't quite remember when or where. Steve's boss recognizes her immediately. Ellen was the driver of a car that nearly ran him off the road earlier that day. Needless to say, it's going to take a lot before the boss can **warm up to** her.

_____

_____

_____

_____

_____

COMMUNICATION   Read and discuss the following.

1. Think of a time when you **gave someone a rough time** or when someone **gave you a hard time.** What happened?

2. *A smile can go a long way.* This expression means that people who take a friendly approach in dealing with others are more likely to get what they want than those who don't. Can you think of a time when a smile made a difference?

3. Think of a time when someone **wouldn't give you the time of day.** How can you explain that person's behavior? How did you respond to it?

4. Perhaps you noticed that warmth is sometimes associated with friendliness (as in **warm up to someone, give someone a warm welcome**) and coolness is sometimes associated with its opposite (as in **be cool toward someone, give someone the cold shoulder**). Why do you suppose this is so? Does temperature have similar associations in your language? If so, share some examples with your classmates.

5. Choose the following saying, or choose a saying or quotation that appeared earlier in the unit. Explain its meaning, or think of a situation that illustrates it.

> *A friend to all is a friend to none.*
> **Greek proverb**

13 Happiness

feel blue   long face

feel down   walk on air

be down in the dumps

be in seventh heaven

be on cloud nine

be on top of the world

be tickled pink

feel like a million bucks

look like one lost one's best friend

WARM-UP

Make a list of special days and events in your country that are associated with feelings of happiness or sadness. Explain to your classmates what makes these days/events happy or sad.

Happy Days/Events

_____

_____

_____

_____

Sad Days/Events

_____

_____

_____

_____

SITUATION

Read or listen to the following passage.

Jim Weaver had achieved happiness by many people's standards. By age 45, he had risen to the position of executive vice president at a major corporation. Jim was very good at his job. What many of Jim's colleagues didn't know was that Jim never liked his job much. In fact, he had always wanted to be a writer. After discussing the situation with his wife and family, Jim decided to quit his job. The Weavers had to adjust their standard of living drastically because now they had only one paycheck to live on instead of two. The first thing they did was to sell their house and move into a smaller one.

Most people had trouble understanding Jim's decision, but his family and friends understood. Almost immediately, they noticed a big change in Jim's attitude. Before, he often seemed to **be down in the dumps**. He didn't seem to enjoy his life much. Nowadays, Jim looks like he **is on top of the world** even though he hasn't published anything he's written yet.

ANALYSIS & EXPLANATION

Circle the best answer to the question below. Then turn to the appendix, where each answer is explained. If your choice is incorrect, choose again.

Why did Jim decide to quit his job?

A. He no longer needed to work at a job that paid a lot of money because he and his wife had enough to live comfortably.

B. After working for many years at the same job, Jim had grown tired of it and he wanted to try something different.

C. He thought his new career would be more satisfying than his former one was.

ATTITUDE

Jim believes that people should strive to attain happiness, a positive mental state that results from the attainment or possession of what people consider to be good.

EXPANSION A

The following situations describe people who feel happy or sad. Write *H* if the idiom expresses Happiness. Write *S* if the idiom expresses Sadness.

S   Jane applied for admission to five universities. Only one of them accepted her. Jane **was down in the dumps** for several days, but then she became her normal, cheerful self again.

S   1. Yesterday, Randy **looked like he lost his best friend**. He is a candidate for mayor and until yesterday it appeared that he had a good chance of winning. However, the latest opinion polls show that he is now in last place. Election day is in two days.

H   2. When Debbie found a wallet that someone had dropped on the sidewalk, she immediately turned it in to the police. Several days later, Debbie got a thank-you note in the mail along with a check for $50. Debbie was **walking on air** for the rest of the day.

S   3. Sue had a ticket to a concert where Whitney Dallas, her favorite recording artist, was appearing. In today's newspaper it was announced that the concert will be cancelled because Whitney is sick. Sue has been walking around with a **long face** ever since.

H   4. Marge **is on cloud nine**. She bought five raffle tickets for a cruise to the Carribean. She has just learned that she won the cruise!

WALK ON AIR

H   5. Ken **is in seventh heaven**. He advertised that he was selling his house for $125,000 and within three days, someone offered him that amount. Ken didn't think the house would sell so soon and for the full asking price.

S   6. Sam has just left his doctor's office where he had his annual physical exam. The doctor told Sam that he was overweight, had high blood pressure, and had a high cholesterol level. Sam is **feeling down**.

S   7. Mary is **feeling blue**. She bought one of those cheap airline tickets that can't be refunded and can't be changed in any way. Today her boss told her that her request for vacation had been denied.

H   8. Philip is the chef and owner of a small restaurant in a large city. The restaurant only opened a few months ago, so it hasn't seen much business yet. Today, Philip learned that the food critic of the city's most influential newspaper will write a very favorable review of the restaurant. Philip **is on top of the world**.

H   9. Kay **feels like a million bucks**. For many years, she suffered from an allergy that made her life miserable. Now, her doctor has found an effective treatment. No more uncontrollable sneezing for Kay.

H   10. Jay **was tickled pink** to hear that his painting had been chosen to be part of the permanent collection in the state museum of art. Only a few artists have been honored in this way.

EXPANSION B

Read each of the following situations. Then respond to the last statement in each situation; write *A* for Agree or *D* for Disagree.

_D_   All her life, Mary wanted to become a pilot. To qualify, she had to have a physical examination. The results of her eye test showed that her vision was very poor. Mary **was tickled pink**.

_a_   1. Bill's friends passed their driving test the first time they took it. Bill failed his test because he didn't bring his car to a complete stop at a traffic intersection. Bill is **feeling down**.

_a_   2. Nicole needed a 600 on the TOEFL in order to be accepted to law school. Earlier today, the results came in the mail. Her score was higher than she needed. Nicole **is on cloud nine**.

_d_   3. Sally has trained for months to run in the Boston Marathon. Two days before the race, she fell down. Her doctor's diagnosis was a twisted ankle. Sally **feels like a million bucks**.

_d_   4. Jay entered one of his paintings in an exhibition. Although Jay didn't expect to win anything, the judges announced that his painting was awarded an honorable mention. Jay **was down in the dumps**.

_a_   5. Debbie got a notice from the Internal Revenue Service stating that she had underpaid her federal taxes by more than $400. Debbie rechecked her tax forms and discovered that she had made a math mistake. Debbie will have to borrow the money. She **looks like she lost her best friend**.

_a_   6. Andy applied for a bank loan to buy a house. He just finished meeting with the loan officer who told him that his application was denied. Andy is **feeling blue**.

_d_   7. Barb has a pet cat named Tabby. Yesterday, the cat ran out the door when Barb opened it. She's looked everywhere but still can't find Tabby. Barb is **walking on air.**

_d_   8. John had an economy ticket for a flight to Philadelphia. When he went to the check-in counter at the airport, the agent told him that the economy seats were overbooked. The agent gave John a seat in first class for the same price. John had a **long face.**

_a_   9. On the advice of a friend who works on Wall Street, Ann emptied her bank account and bought 500 shares of a major computer company. Within a week, the price of the stock had doubled. Ann **was on top of the world.**

_a_   10. Ralph has less than a month to go before he retires. He plans to move to Florida where he has bought a condo. Ralph **is in seventh heaven.**

EXPANSION C

Imagine that you are the person who is described in the sentences below. Use idioms from this unit to explain your feelings or the feelings of others in each of the following situations.

You are leaving soon for a month-long vacation. You are now passing through the departure gate at the airport. You turn around and wave goodbye to the friend who came to see you off. Your friend seems sad to see you leave.

My friend _is feeling blue_ .

1. You have just boarded the plane. You are spending the next three weeks on Tahiti in a first-class hotel that overlooks the beach. This is the vacation you have dreamed about for years.

   I _____ .

2. Unfortunately, the plane is delayed in taking off. The plane sits on the runway for twenty minutes. The temperature inside the cabin gets hotter and hotter. You break out into a sweat. You feel a headache coming on.

   I _____ .

3. Finally, the plane takes off and soon reaches cruising altitude. The flight attendants serve beverages and snacks. You begin to relax again. You are having pleasant thoughts of Tahiti. You can almost hear the rolling waves and the swaying palm trees. You smile to yourself.

   I _____ .

4. Several hours later, you finish dinner. One of the attendants announces that the film will soon begin. You put on the headset and watch. You become interested in one of the main characters, a person whose life reminds you of a friend. The friend moved away last year and it is unlikely that you will ever see each other again.

   I _____ .

5. After the film, the attendant turns the cabin lights down low. Some of the other passengers are already asleep, but you are not tired at all. You switch on the overhead light and begin reading a newspaper. You check the financial pages to see how your investments are doing. You notice a story about a company whose stock you own. The company has declared record profits.

   I _____ .

6. You've been flying now for six hours. You are starting to get drowsy. You fall asleep. You begin to dream about your first evening in Tahiti. You meet someone who is good-looking, charming, and rich. You have dinner by candlelight together and go for a walk on the beach afterward. There is a full moon.

   I _____ .

7. You wake up because the plane is experiencing some turbulence. You and the person sitting next to you start talking. She tells you that the airline had lost her suitcase. In the suitcase was the only copy of a manuscript she had been working on for months.

She _____ .

8. Soon the plane starts its descent. The passengers are asked to return the seats to their original, upright positions and to make sure that their seatbelts are fastened. You look out the window and see land. It's your first glimpse of Tahiti!

I _____ .

9. At the end of three wonderful weeks, you find yourself back at the airport. You are about to board a flight to go home. You have mixed feelings. On one hand, you are looking forward to seeing your family and friends again. On the other hand, you aren't ready for your vacation to end yet.

I _____

but I also _____

_____

_____ .

> *After you have traveled the whole world, you learn that happiness is to be found only in your own home.*
>
> **Voltaire**

> *Happiness is the only thing we can give without having.*
>
> **Anonymous**

> *The search for happiness is one of the chief sources of unhappiness.*
>
> **Eric Hoffer**

EXPANSION D

Use one or two idioms from this unit to explain your reactions to the following news.

The good news is that the coat that was too expensive to buy is on sale! The bad news is that the sale ended yesterday.

At first I was on top of the world, but then I was feeling down.

1. The good news is that you won a vacation on a cruise ship that will take you to the Greek Islands! The bad news is that you get seasick easily.

   _____

2. The good news is that you found a $50 bill on the sidewalk today! The bad news is that it's counterfeit.

   _____

3. The good news is that you think you did very well on the TOEFL! The bad news is that the Educational Testing Service invalidated all the scores and you will have to retake the test.

   _____

4. The good news is that you got a 10% pay increase this year! The bad news is that everyone else in your office got more.

   _____

5. The good news is that today is your birthday! The bad news is that no one remembered.

   _____

6. The good news is that you won 10 gallons of ice cream in a drawing! The bad news is that it's the middle of the coldest winter in years.

   _____

7. The good news is that someone found and returned your missing wallet! The bad news is that all the cash, credit cards, and IDs are missing.

   _____

8. The good news is that you had a dental checkup and you had no cavities! The bad news is that the office visit cost you $200.

   _____

9. The good news is that you are going to visit your favorite relatives for a weekend! The bad news is that they have a cat and you are allergic to cats.

   _____

10. The good news is that today you got a long letter from home! No bad news.

   _____

COMMUNICATION   **Read and discuss the following.**

1. Happiness for many Americans is thought to be possible by achieving *the good life,* a lifestyle characterized by a high standard of living. Do you think that happiness depends to some degree upon having material comforts? Is it possible to buy happiness?

2. Feelings of happiness are sometimes expressed with words that indicate an upward direction, while feelings of sadness are sometimes expressed with words that indicate a downward direction. Identify the idioms in this unit that do this. Why do you suppose these two directions are associated with feelings of happiness and sadness?

3. On July 4, 1776, representatives from thirteen colonies in North America signed a document that declared the colonies to be independent from Great Britain. The United States Declaration of Independence identifies a number of *inalienable rights* (rights that are inherent and absolute) for all people. One right is the *pursuit of happiness.* Do you agree that the pursuit of happiness is an inalienable right?

4. Do people in your country associate certain numbers with feelings of happiness or sadness? For example, Moslems believe that Allah and the most exalted angels live in seventh heaven.

5. Choose one of the following sayings or quotations, or choose one that appeared earlier in the unit. Explain its meaning, or think of a situation that illustrates it.

> *Much happiness is overlooked because it doesn't cost much.*
>
> *Anonymous*

> *Happiness? That's nothing more than good health and a poor memory.*
>
> *Albert Schweitzer*

Limitations

14

take it easy   *hands are full*

run oneself ragged   *be in over one's head*

be stretched to the limit

bite off more than one can chew

burn the candle at both ends

can't do everything at once

eyes are bigger than one's stomach

feel as if one is being pulled in a hundred/ thousand/million different directions

have more work than one can handle

spread oneself too thin

WARM-UP

Burnout is a condition that is characterized by physical or emotional exhaustion, especially as a result of long-term stress. Certain occupations are associated with this condition, including the ones listed below. Add to the list if you can, and explain why you think these occupations often involve burnout.

fire fighters   _____

police officers   _____

air traffic controllers   _____

teachers   _____

assembly-line workers   _____

_____   _____

Antonio Vallente and his brother Giuseppe own and operate a popular restaurant that is open every day except Mondays. Every morning, Antonio goes to market to buy fresh food. Afternoons are spent cooking. On most evenings, they don't close until after ten o'clock. And then there's the cleaning up that has to be done. Even with a staff of two waiters, Antonio and Giuseppe are lucky if they can get home by midnight.

Giuseppe went to Italy last month to visit his family. Antonio has been doing the work of two people, and it is beginning to wear him down. Giuseppe isn't expected back for another three weeks. Today is Monday, so the restaurant is closed. Antonio is at home with his wife, Francesca.

Francesca: Are you all right, Antonio? You don't look so good.

Antonio: Oh, I'm OK. A little tired maybe. That's all. I just need to get a good night's sleep and I'll be fine.

Francesca: I think you need a lot more than that. You'**re running yourself ragged** at work. You can't go on like this.

Antonio: It won't be much longer. Guiseppe will be back in a couple of weeks.

Francesca: Not a couple—three. You won't last that long. Even when he's here, you two **have more work than you can handle**. Why don't you let me help? Things are slow at the office. I can probably take some time off from work.

Antonio: Do you think you could stand being around me all day long?

Francesca: There's only one way to find out.

ANALYSIS & EXPLANATION

Circle the best answer to the question below. Then turn to the appendix, where each answer is explained. If your choice is incorrect, choose again.

Why did Francesca volunteer to help Antonio?

A. She doesn't get to see him very much because he is so busy, and this would be one way to spend more time with him.

B. She thinks he has obligated himself to do more work than he has time for or can accomplish well.

C. She is worried that the quality of service at the restaurant will suffer if her husband doesn't get someone to help him.

ATTITUDE

Francesca thinks that her husband should know what his limitations are, and he should not exceed them.

EXPANSION A

Read the following story and write an ending.

Maria Lucia is a graduate business student from Brazil. She also teaches Portuguese on the side. When she agreed to teach, she had no idea that she might **be in over her head**. Now, she is finally beginning to realize that she might **be burning the candle at both ends.** If she's not in class, she's studying for class. If she's not studying for class, she is teaching class. In short, Maria **is running herself ragged**. Her friends worry that if she continues to **spread herself too thin**, she might fail her classes and lose her job.

At the end of her first semester at school, Maria was using her computer to finish up a term paper. She had spent a lot of time researching and writing this paper. Only one more page to go, and then she would be able to **take it easy** for a while. Just then, the computer *crashed,* meaning that the entire system stopped and all work in progress was lost.

Maria was frantic. She got out her user's guide, and read the section on troubleshooting. Pretty soon she realized that she had **bitten off more than she could chew**, so she decided to get professional help. She called a local computer dealer and described the problem. Mike, who works in the repairs department, told her that this often happens when a computer's memory **is stretched to the limit**. Maria asked if she could bring in her computer right away for a memory upgrade, but Mike told her that he **had more work than he could handle** that day. Maria explained why she needed repairs done urgently. Mike laughed and said that everyone wants him to drop whatever he is doing and start working on their computer. He said that he **can't do everything at once**, and these days he **feels like he is being pulled in a thousand different directions**. Maria pleaded with Mike, and told him that...

it is very important for her to get restored the memory of her computer, because she

Too much of a good thing can be wonderful.
Mae West

EXPANSION B

Use an idiom from this unit to describe the person or persons in each of the following situations.

A writer who has three editors. Each one suggests that she change her manuscript in different ways.

She must feel as though she is being pulled in a hundred different directions.

1. A student who registers for five courses, drops one after a couple of weeks, and ends up failing another.

   _____

2. A jogger who runs until her muscles start hurting and then she stops.

   _____

3. A diner who orders several appetizers, a main course, a dessert, and then can't finish them.

   _____

4. An employee who has to come to the office on weekends to catch up on all the office work.

   _____

5. A woman who is raising two childen, employed fulltime, and working on a graduate degree—all at the same time. It's tough, but she's able to do it all.

   _____

6. A waiter who has ten tables to look after, all of which are full. Everybody has finished eating about the same time and they want their checks.

   _____

7. A professor who promised his students on a Friday he would read their research reports and return them the following Monday. It is Sunday night and he still has 25 papers to read.

   _____

8. A musical group that is on tour. Their agent booked them to perform in a different city every other night for a month.

   _____

9. A secretary who works straight through the day without taking lunch or any coffee breaks because the other secretary has called in sick.

   _____

10. A host who expected ten people for dinner, but fourteen came. Even so, there will be just enough food for everyone.

_____

11. A stockbroker who works twelve hours a day, six days a week.

_____

12. A school guidance counselor who meets with twenty students every day, and who serves as advisor to the student newspaper and the yearbook.

_____

EXPANSION C   Refer to the events in the Situation and in Expansion A to complete the following activities. Use idioms from this unit in your answers.

1. Suppose that Francesca is at home and receives a telephone call from Italy. It's Giuseppe and he is having a wonderful time on vacation—so wonderful, in fact, that he would like to stay a few more weeks. What can Francesca say to encourage him to return home?

2. Suppose that Maria Lucia was able to get her computer repaired, but she discovered that the file containing most of her research term paper was lost. She had to start all over again, and in consequence she wasn't able to finish on time. When she turned in her paper, she attached a note to her professor. What might the note have said?

EXPANSION D   Write five statements in which you describe unusual or interesting things that have happened to you. Three or more of the statements must be true, but one or two can be false. When you finish writing your statements, tell them to your classmates and see if they can guess which of your statements are false. Use one idiom from this unit in each of your statements.

_____

_____

_____

_____

_____

COMMUNICATION   Read and discuss the following.

1. If you are asked to do something in less time than you are able to do it, you can say, "There are only so many hours in a day." If you are asked to do more work than can reasonably be done by one person, then you can say, "There's only so much one person can do." Think of a request for which it would be appropriate to respond with each of these expressions.

2. A *doggy bag* is a small bag provided upon request by a restaurant for a customer to carry home leftovers of a meal. The contents of the bag may end up as food for a dog or pet, but it is more likely that the food will be eaten by the customer or another person. Doggy bags are often requested by customers whose **eyes are bigger than their stomachs**. Do restaurants provide doggy bags in your country? If so, what are they called? If not, what would the reaction probably be if someone asked for one?

3. Choose one of the following quotations, or choose one that appeared earlier in the unit. Explain its meaning, or think of a situation that illustrates it.

> *I think knowing what you cannot do is more important than knowing what you can do.*
> *Lucille Ball*

> *In everything the middle course is best: all things in excess bring trouble.*
> *Plautus*

Humility 15

show off put on airs

be stuck up eat humble pie

be down to earth

be too big for one's britches

go to one's head

have a swollen head

put someone in someone's place

swallow one's pride

take someone down a notch/peg or two

toot one's own horn

WARM-UP

You probably have met someone who is *pretentious*. A person who assumes an air of superiority in order to impress others is a pretentious person. You probably also have met someone who is *humble*. A person who has no pretensions is a modest or humble person. These two types of people would react very differently to the same situation. What might a pretentious person say after winning a competition? What might a humble person say?

_____

_____

_____

Ed is the star of his high school's basketball team. Ed is so good that coaches from many major universities have visited the school to recruit Ed to play on their teams after he graduates from high school. At first, Ed was unaffected by all the attention, but lately he seems different. At least, that's what two of his teammates think.

John: I wish the old Ed would come back.

Mark: I think I know what you mean. He sure has changed.

John: Ed's favorite topic these days is Ed.

Mark: Favorite? You mean his only topic.

John: I swear if I hear him tell us one more time how fantastic he is, I'll go crazy. I wonder if he knows how many friends he's lost because of his new attitude.

Mark: Yesterday he gave Ann one of those autographed photographs of himself. He told her to hold on to it because it will be worth a lot of money some day soon. If I thought he was joking, it would be OK, but he really believes it. This whole thing has **gone to his head**.

John: I hate to say this, but I almost wish he'd lose once in a while. Nothing permanent, just long enough to **put him in his place**.

Mark: Yeah, it's not healthy for him to be so preoccupied with himself.

John: It isn't good for the team either.

ANALYSIS & EXPLANATION

Circle the best answer to the question below. Then turn to the appendix, where each answer is explained. If your choice is incorrect, choose again.

Which of the following best describes how John and Mark now feel toward Ed?

A. They are jealous of Ed's success and all the attention that he is getting.

B. They are worried that Ed will continue to lose his friends unless he changes his attitude.

C. They are upset that success and its accompanying attention has inflated Ed's opinion of himself.

ATTITUDE

John and Mark believe that people should not hold an excessively high opinion of their own importance. They feel a person should display some modesty.

EXPANSION A

If the person in each of the following situations shows modesty, put a plus sign (+) in the blank. If not, put a minus sign (-).

____+____ A colleague at work was recently promoted. Before his promotion, he was very friendly to everyone in the office. Now, he refuses to associate with people whose status is lower than his. He has let his promotion **go to his head**. That is, he has an inflated sense of self-importance.

____ 1. A famous author of mystery books was seen autographing a copy of her novel. Not only did she sign the book, she spent a few minutes chatting with the person who bought it. The author **is down to earth**. That is, she doesn't see herself as special or privileged.

____ 2. A customer in a restaurant was observed snapping her fingers at the waiters and flashing a handful of money. She was **putting on airs**. That is, her behavior was an offensive display of superiority over others.

____ 3. A well-known scholar has just published a book. Looking at the reference section at the back of the book, a colleague noticed that Adams had cited himself many times. When the colleague mentioned this, Adams responded that he had an obligation to cite the very best sources! Adams **has a swollen head**. That is, he thinks he is better than others.

____ 4. A lawyer had the habit of reminding his friends that he worked for one of the best law firms in the country. Recently, the firm lost several very important cases which they argued in court. When his friends kidded him about this, the lawyer had to **eat humble pie**. That is, he had to admit publicly that he was wrong, and this embarrassed him.

_____ 5. Soon after announcing that she had discovered a cure for a tropical disease, a noted biochemist **swallowed her pride** and admitted that her research was flawed. That is, she brought embarrassment to herself by publicly admitting her mistake.

_____ 6. A teenage guy who has a new expensive sports car keeps driving it up and down a block where lots of other teenagers spend time. He's **showing off** his new car. That is, he is trying to attract attention to his car because he is especially proud of it.

_____ 7. After a girl in the third grade won a spelling contest in her class, she began to correct everyone's mistakes in English. Her teacher decided that the girl **was too big for her britches**. That is, the teacher thought that her student was exaggerating her own importance.

_____ 8. The parents of a college student disapproved of her marriage to a man whose family had no money and no social position. The parents **are stuck-up**. That is, they believe themselves to be better than others.

_____ 9. At a job interview, an applicant was asked what she did best. She answered that she was excellent at identifying and solving problems. She **was tooting her own horn**. That is, she was talking about her own talents and achievements.

_____ 10. A newspaper reporter said that news stories always won awards because of luck, not talent and hard work. After the same reporter won a prize for one of his stories, he told his co-workers that hard work and talent were responsible, and that luck had nothing to do with him winning the prize. The co-workers think someone should **take him down a notch or two** or that someone should **put him in his place**. That is, they think someone should do or say something to the reporter that would have the effect of lowering his pride or self-importance.

> *It is well to remember that the entire population of the universe, with one trifling exception, is composed of others.*
> *John Andrew Holmes*

> *At home I am a nice guy, but I don't want the world to know. Humble people, I've found, don't get very far.*
> *Mohammad Ali*

EXPANSION B

Answer the question at the end of each situation below with *yes* or *no*.

_no_   Mary can afford to hire people to take care of all her needs, but she still likes to do a lot of the housework herself. Has Mary let money **go to her head**?

_____   1. Rob often makes comments about how good-looking and popular he is. Does Rob **have a swollen head**?

_____   2. Linda came in first in the school tennis championship. When her friends congratulated her, she told them it was pure luck. Was Linda **tooting her own horn**?

_____   3. Cindy got an autograph of a famous film star. To hear her talk now, you would think that she and the star are best of friends. Is Cindy **putting on airs**?

_____   4. Stan is the president of a company that employs about two hundred people. Stan greets all of his employees by their first name and expects them to do the same to him. **Is** Stan **stuck up**?

_____   5. Ken won a spelling contest. When he walked to the stage to receive his prize, he seemed ill at ease because he wasn't used to so much attention. Is Ken **showing off**?

_____   6. Sam was bragging to his friends that he was a better athlete than they were. Mary challenged him to a race and she beat him. Did Mary **put** Sam **in his place**?

_____   7. When Sue complimented Bill on the expert job he did in repairing her broken watch, he said, "It was nothing. Fixing things comes natural to me." **Is** Bill **too big for his britches**?

_____   8. Rob is a senior at college. He and his roommate were recently discussing the qualities they were looking for in a relationship. Rob's roommate said he was looking for honesty and sincerity. Rob said that the person had to be at least as good-looking and intelligent as he was. Does Rob need to be **taken down a peg or two**?

_____   9. Linda is treasurer of a civic organization. At a meeting of the officers, she said that the treasury was full and there was no need to raise membership dues. A week later, she bounced a check drawn on the organization's account. Did Linda have to **eat humble pie**?

_____   10. John has been introduced several times to Angela, but Angela always acts as though she has never seen him before. When John asked her why she ignores him, Angela told him that he didn't have the "right" social background. **Is** Angela **down to earth**?

_____   11. Everyone including Sandy thought that she would win the tennis championship. After all, she had won the past two years and her challenger was not rated very highly. In an upset, the challenger won a stunning victory. Did Sandy have to **swallow her pride**?

EXPANSION C

Using idioms from this unit, first describe Evelyn, then describe Ron, or describe what happened to both of them.

A few weeks ago, there was a major blowup in my office. I have a very responsible position in a large brokerage firm. My job is to act as an agent for people who want to buy or sell stock certificates. A new customer came in last week asking for some investment advice. This person was obviously very rich, a high society type. She acted like a real snob. Her name, by the way, was Evelyn Denault. My name is Ron Culp, and it's written in very large letters on a plaque that sits on my desk in plain view. Evelyn kept butchering my name. First, she called me Don, then Tom, and finally John. This really annoyed me, but I tried to overlook it. After all, she was a customer. Next, she asked me what my position with the company was. When I told her I was an account executive, she said she couldn't possibly do business with anyone who was less than a vice president. That did it for me. I asked her how much money she planned to invest, and she said $50,000. I told her that I couldn't possibly do business with anyone who wasn't prepared to invest at least a half million. I was lying, of course, but I didn't care. This person really was impossible to deal with. Anyway, unfortunately for me, my boss overheard the entire conversation. That was the blowup I mentioned. In the end, I had to apologize to Ms. Denault. I did, but I was terribly embarrassed. The apology didn't do any good. Evelyn took her money elsewhere.

_____

_____

_____

_____

_____

_____

_____

_____

_____

_____

> *I want to thank you for stopping the applause. It is impossible for me to look humble for any period of time.*
>
> **Henry Kissinger**

EXPANSION D

Refer to the events in the Situation to complete the following activities. Use idioms from this unit in your answers.

1. Later the same day, Ann runs into John. John mentions that he heard about the autographed photograph. Ann takes the opportunity to let John know exactly what she thinks of Ed. What might she say?

2. The next time the team gets together for practice, Ed starts boasting that his teammates should consider themselves lucky that they have the opportunity to play with him. That comment is all that John needs to hear. (Remember that John told Mark he would "go crazy" if he heard Ed talk about how fantastic he was one more time.) John waits until after practice, and then he goes up to Ed. What might he say?

3. Ed's coach is aware of what is happening. He knows that Ed's attitude is having a negative effect on the rest of the team. He calls Ed in for a talk. What might he say?

4. After both John and the coach talk to Ed, he realizes his mistake and he agrees to the coach's suggestion that he apologize to the team. The next day in the locker room, Ed tells his teammates that he has something important he wants to say. What might he say next?

BE TOO BIG FOR ONE'S BRITCHES

1. American boxer Mohammad Ali (born in 1942 as Cassius Clay) won an Olympic gold medal in 1960 and the world heavyweight crown in 1964, 1974, and again in 1978. Ali's style in the boxing ring is remembered as much as his style outside the ring. During interviews with the press, he often would boast, "I am the greatest!" Using what you have learned in this unit, comment on Ali's behavior.

2. Long ago, servants at hunting feasts were given a kind of pie made with *numbles,* an archaic word that referred to the less choice parts of an animal, especially a deer. It is thought that perhaps the term *humble pie* originated with the term *numbles pie.* Why might people think this is so?

3. The verbs *humble* and *humiliate* are derived from the same root although an important distinction exists in their meanings. If A humbles B, then A reduces the pride of B. If A humiliates B, then A makes B feel inadequate or unworthy, especially in some public setting. Describe a situation in which one of the following happened: (1) someone humiliated you; (2) you humiliated someone; (3) you saw or heard about someone who humiliated someone else.

4. If you compliment or praise someone you know well, you might then say to that person, "Don't let it **go to your head**." This expression tends to diminish the praise by reminding us to keep a balanced sense of self-importance. Choose several classmates and say something highly complimentary to each one and then say, "Don't let it **go to your head**."

5. Think of someone you know (or know of) and explain how that person let power, fame, money, or success **go to his/her head**.

6. Choose one of the quotations that appeared earlier in the unit. Explain its meaning, or think of a situation that illustrates it.

16 Harmony

get along   make waves

rock the boat   see eye to eye

flow with the tide

forgive and forget

have a bone to pick with someone

let bygones be bygones

let sleeping dogs lie

make a federal case out of something

open a can of worms

upset the applecart

WARM-UP

An *idiosyncrasy* is a characteristic, habit, or mannerism that is peculiar to a person. Everyone has idiosyncratic behaviors. Some of them may be cute, but some may be annoying. An example of an annoying habit might be if people talk when their mouths are full.

Make a list of five idiosyncrasies that you would find annoying in a close friend. Compare your list with that of a classmate. Discuss whether you would tolerate these idiosyncrasies for the sake of harmony in your relationship, or whether you would try to change them.

SITUATION

Read or listen to the following passage.

Harold and Maude are grandparents to Timmy, who just turned five. Timmy and his parents, Peg and Mark, live down the street so Harold and Maude often see them. This morning, Harold walked downtown to cash a check. Maude wanted to spend the morning planning a luncheon she is giving for some friends.

Harold: Honey, I'm back.

Maude: And not a minute too soon.

Harold: What do you mean?

Maude: Take a look in the living room.

Harold: What happened in here? It looks like a hurricane hit.

Maude: Exactly. Hurricane Timmy paid us a visit.

Harold: Where is our little bundle of joy now?

Maude: Upstairs sleeping, and let's hope he stays that way. Peg stopped by about an hour ago and dropped him off. She's getting her hair done.

Harold: I don't remember her saying anything about a hair appointment.

Maude: She didn't, and I didn't get a thing done this morning on my luncheon. You know, this is the second time this week she's done this. I don't want to **make a federal case out of this**, but I wish she would be a little more considerate of us. We've got our lives, too. I suppose she thinks that because we're retired, we've got all the time in the world.

Harold: You wouldn't want her to think we don't enjoy taking care of Timmy. Maybe we should just **let sleeping dogs lie**.

Maude: She knows we enjoy having Timmy over. I still think there has to be some way we can let her know that it's not always convenient for us to babysit.

ANALYSIS & EXPLANATION

Circle the best answer to the question below. Then turn to the appendix, where each answer is explained. If your choice is incorrect, choose again.

Why does Harold think Maude probably shouldn't say anything to Peg?

A. Peg might conclude that they don't enjoy Timmy's visits.
B. The issue isn't important enough to risk damaging their relationship.
C. Timmy might overhear them talking about him.

ATTITUDE

Harold and Maude value the good relationship they have with Peg. They are reluctant to do or say anything that will jeopardize relations with their daughter if they can avoid it.

EXPANSION A

Read the following passage, putting yourself in the shoes of each of the characters. Discuss with your classmates how you would have reacted to each of the events.

An hour or so later, Peg got back from her hair appointment. She asked if Timmy had behaved himself, and Maude told her he was a perfect angel. She decided not to tell her that Timmy had bumped up against a coffee table, and had knocked over and broken an expensive crystal bowl. **Making a federal case out of** the broken bowl wouldn't bring it back. No, it was better to **let bygones be bygones**. Peg went upstairs and got Timmy. As they were leaving Maude and Harold's house, Peg waved to their next door neighbor, Ben Hornby. Ben, who was out raking leaves, smiled and waved back.

Ben **gets along** very well with Harold and Maude. However, he does **have one bone to pick with them**. He wishes they would help him rake up all those leaves. The leaves come from a big old tree that is on Harold and Maude's property. Every time the wind starts blowing, the leaves fall on his lawn. Ben really resents that he has to pick them all up. Rather than **rock the boat**, however, he decides not to say anything.

In the house on the other side of Ben lives Mark Rentz. On most weekends, Mark entertains on his back porch by inviting friends over for a barbecue. Mark and Ben **see eye to eye** on most matters, but there is one small but noisy thing that bothers Mark a lot about Ben: his dog. It barks non-stop, and the noise always ruins his barbecues. Many times he has wanted to have a word with Ben about his dog, but he knows that would be **opening a can of worms**, so he always ends up deciding not to say anything. Why **make waves** if you don't have to?

LET SLEEPING DOGS LIE

Next door to Mark lives Ann Stubbs. Ann has had Mark over to her house for dinner several times, but Mark has never invited her to any of his barbecues. Ann was willing to **forgive and forget** the first time this happened, but now she's not likely to **let sleeping dogs lie**. The next time Mark has one of his barbecues, she is going to **upset the applecart** and drop by. At least that's what Ann says she'll do.

Next door to Ann on the corner lot lives Jill Wang. Jill **gets along** well with Ann, except for one small matter. Ann always puts her trash out on the corner a couple of days before pickup. Ben's dog invariably eats through the plastic bag, and trash gets all over Ann's lawn. Usually Ann **flows with the tide**, but this time she is determined to say something.

My idea of an agreeable person is a person who agrees with me.
                                        Benjamin Disraeli

EXPANSION B

Use idioms from this unit to describe the people and events in the following story.

Every summer, the Bumpus family gets together for a reunion. Like most families, some members **get along**, and some do not. Last year, Uncle Harry and Uncle Bill had a big fight because Uncle Harry smashed up Uncle Bill's car. This year, things seem to be a lot better. At least they're smiling at each other. Aunt Evelyn, though, was in a terrible mood and managed to insult just about everyone. She really picked on Uncle John. She told him he was a good-for-nothing bum, and that if she had known he was coming to the picnic she wouldn't have come. Jan was there with her new husband, Jay. Everyone wanted to meet him. Jan and Jay seem perfectly suited to each other. They seem to agree on just about everything.

Uncle Frank and Aunt Mary are still fighting. We were all eating hamburgers and hot dogs and having a good time when Uncle Frank helped himself to some of Aunt Mary's potato salad. After eating a bite, he said in a voice that everyone could hear that it was the worst potato salad he had ever eaten in his whole life. No one came to Aunt Mary's defense. The potato salad really was pretty bad.

Just as it was getting dark, we all said goodbye and went home. I wonder who will be talking to each other next year. These family reunions are such fun!

_____

_____

_____

_____

_____

_____

_____

_____

_____

_____

> *One person gets nothing but discord out of a piano; another gets harmony. No one claims that the piano is at fault. Life is about the same. The discord is there, and the harmony is there, too. Study to play it correctly, and it will give forth the beauty. Play it falsely, and it will give forth ugliness. Life is not at fault.*
>
> *Anonymous*

EXPANSION C Discuss with a classmate what you would do in each of the following situations. Use idioms from this unit in your answer.

1. You planned a surprise party for a friend. One of the people you invited ruined the surprise by letting out the secret.

2. A police officer pulls you over for speeding, but in fact you were not.

3. Your neighbor's dog keeps digging up your lawn to bury bones in it.

4. All of your friends want to spend the weekend in the mountains, but you want to go to the beach.

5. You and someone special go to dinner at an expensive restaurant. You had made a reservation two weeks ago. When you get to the restaurant, you are told that they have no record of your reservation, and there's no chance you can be seated that evening.

6. You suspect that someone living in your dorm is a thief.

7. Everyone in your class wants to start class a half hour earlier. You are the only one who can't come at that time.

8. Your roommate frequently gets phone calls late at night. Your roommate stays up late, but you like to turn in early.

9. You are cooking a meal and your roommate/friend/spouse keeps coming in the kitchen and offering unwelcome suggestions.

10. A friend borrowed a few dollars from you and promised to pay you back, but never did. This same friend has asked you for more money.

EXPANSION D Work with a classmate to complete the following roleplay. One of you is someone having marital difficulties, and one of you is a friend. Decide which role you will play, and read only the paragraph that describes your role.

Spouse: You are about to break up with your spouse. You don't **see eye to eye** on anything at all. You tell your friend all about it. In the end, you expect sympathy from your friend and support for your decision to seek a divorce.

Friend: You have seen too many friends go through divorces, and you are not going to let it happen to this marriage. No matter what your friend says, you will try to talk him/her into giving the marriage a second chance. You think your friend should **let bygones be bygones**.

> *It is my melancholy fate to like so many people*
> *I profoundly disagree with, and heartily*
> *dislike many people who agree with me.*
> *Mary Kingsley*

1. When two surfaces come into contact, the force that resists motion is called *friction*. Apart from its technical use in physics, friction also can refer to conflict that occurs between people who have differing ideas, wishes, or interests, as in the following sentences:

   > There is always friction when those two get together.
   > Did you notice any friction between them?

   In physics, it is impossible to eliminate friction. The best that can be done is to reduce it. What about in human relations? Do you think people can live without friction? Is harmony really possible?

2. There are times when people do not value harmony over conflict. In fact, sometimes, people actually seem to want to fight, as can be seen in the following idioms:

   > Are you *looking for trouble*?
   > Are you trying to *pick a fight*?

   Ask several classmates about a time when they or someone they know *went looking for trouble* or *picked a fight*. What happened?

3. Sometimes, people *look for trouble* or *pick fights* by exaggerating the importance of a trivial complaint, as in **make a federal case out of something**, or in the following two idioms:

   > You're *making a mountain out of a molehill.*
   > You're trying to *make a big deal out of nothing.*

   Give an example of a time when someone tried to *make a mountain out of a molehole.*

4. Do you think it always is wise to adopt a policy of **forgive and forget**? If not, when isn't it wise?

5. One way of preparing someone for a minor complaint is to say, "I **have a bone to pick with you**," and then state your complaint. For example, you might say to your roommate, "I have a bone to pick with you. You said you would pick up my shirts at the dry cleaners, and you forgot." Can you think of a time when someone **had a bone to pick with you** or when you **had a bone to pick with someone else**? What was it?

6. Choose the following saying, or choose one of the sayings or quotations that appeared earlier in the unit. Explain its meaning, or think of a situation that illustrates it.

   > *If there is harmony in the home, there will be order in the nation. When there is order in the nation, there will be peace in the world.*
   > **Chinese proverb**

Intellectual Competence

17

be out to lunch   *be out in left field*

have a screw loose   *have a lot on the ball*

be (as) sharp as a tack

have a good head on one's shoulders

not have anything between one's ears

not know enough to come in out of the rain

not know whether one is coming or going

pick someone's brain

play with half a deck

put on one's thinking cap

WARM-UP

Make a list of four occupations that you think are intellectually demanding. Compare your list with that of a classmate. Ask your classmate if he/she finds any of your answers to be surprising.

_____

_____

_____

_____

Sally and Bob are sophomores at a large university where they are majoring in journalism. They are having coffee together in the student center. Sally is reading the local newspaper, and Bob is doing his homework.

Sally: You're not going to believe this, Bob. Dr. Rosenfield won a Pulitzer Prize.

Bob: Oh, yeah. I heard all about it on the radio this morning.

Sally: You knew? You actually knew, and you didn't say anything? Unbelievable!

Bob: Sorry. I forgot she's your favorite professor.

Sally: Listen. The paper says it's "in recognition of her accomplishments in American journalism." Do you remember I told you about the article she published on health care for the elderly? That's the article she got the prize for.

Bob: I don't know why you're so surprised. Everyone knows she **has a lot on the ball—** unlike my prof. I sure wish I were in your class.

Sally: Yeah. He **doesn't know whether he's coming or going.**

Bob: Here's the latest. We were supposed to have a test last week, so I stayed up all night studying. I get to class and guess what? No test. He completely forgot about it!

Sally: Maybe you two have more in common than you think.

Bob: What do you mean by that?

Sally: You both seem to be pretty forgetful.

Bob: Hey, I said I was sorry. What else do you want me to say?

Sally: Oh, look who's coming—It's Dr. Rosenfield. I want to run over real quick and congratulate her. I'll be right back. Wait for me.

Circle the best answer to the question below. Then turn to the appendix, where each answer is explained. If your choice is incorrect, choose again.

Why does Bob wish he were in Dr. Rosenfield's class?

A. Because Dr. Rosenfield won a Pulitzer Prize.
B. Because he recognizes that he can learn a lot from Dr. Rosenfield.
C. Because he is interested in health care issues, especially health care for older people.

ATTITUDE

Sally and Bob admire intellectual competence. Intellectual competence involves clear, logical thinking, the accumulation of knowledge, and the ability to apply that knowledge.

EXPANSION A

For each of the following situations, put a plus sign (+) if the idiom illustrates intellectual competence, or a minus sign (-) if it does not.

__+__ Harry **has a lot on the ball**. He was just given a promotion because of his invention.

__+__ 1. John**'s as sharp as a tack**. He graduated first in his class.

__−__ 2. Mary **doesn't have anything between her ears**. She thinks Spain is somewhere in South America.

__−__ 3. Bill is **playing with half a deck**. He wanted to return a pair of pants he bought, but he couldn't remember where he had bought them.

__+__ 4. Julie really **has a good head on her shoulders**. I always ask her for advice when I have a problem.

__−__ 5. Larry **is out to lunch**. Even though it was freezing yesterday, he was outside without a coat.

__−__ 6. Sue **has a screw loose**. She put dinner in the oven hours ago, but forgot to turn the heat on. She can't figure out why it isn't ready to eat yet.

__−__ 7. Greg **is out in left field**. We were talking about the problems of pollution, and he didn't even realize that pollution is a major world concern.

HAVE A LOT ON THE BALL

___ 8. Dave is **putting on his thinking cap**. He is trying to figure out how he can balance his household budget.

___ 9. Margaret **doesn't know enough to come in out of the rain**. She is so distracted that she forgets to look for approaching cars before crossing the street.

___ 10. Marianne **doesn't know whether she is coming or going**. She is a sophomore now and she has already changed her major three times.

___ 11. Linda is **picking Dick's brain**. She wants to buy a computer but doesn't know much about them. Dick is an expert.

> *There is nothing so irritating as somebody with less intelligence and more common sense.*
>
> *Don Herold*

EXPANSION B

Choose the best idiom(s)—a, b, or c—for each of the following situations.

_b, c_   Steve was the first one to finish the exam and he got all the answers correct.
         a. He **is out in left field**.
         b. He **has a good head on his shoulders**.
         c. He **is as sharp as a tack**.

_b_   1. Debbie spent a lot of time studying for her exam but she failed it.
         a. She **has a good head on her shoulders**.
         b. She **doesn't have anything between her ears**.
         c. She **has a lot on the ball**.

_____   2. Bill thought he lost the books he borrowed from the library. He forgot that he had already returned them.
         a. He **doesn't know whether he is coming or going**.
         b. He **doesn't have anything between his ears**.
         c. He **has a good head on his shoulders**.

_____   3. Steve is having trouble with his physics homework. He knows that Mary always gets top grades in physics, so he asks her for help.
         a. He is **picking her brain**.
         b. He **is out to lunch**.
         c. He is **playing with half a deck**.

_____   4. Janice called the police to report that her car had been stolen. It turns out that she had forgotten where she parked it.
         a. She **is out to lunch**.
         b. She **is playing with half a deck**.
         c. She **doesn't know whether she is coming or going**.

_____   5. Mark is at his desk studying.
         a. He **has a screw loose**.
         b. He **is putting on his thinking cap**.
         c. He **doesn't know enough to come in out of the rain**.

_____   6. Barb has a sprained ankle but she is walking on it.
         a. She **is sharp as a tack**.
         b. She **doesn't know enough to come in out of the rain**.
         c. She **has a screw loose**.

> *I not only use all the brains I have, but all the brains I can borrow.*
>
>   *Woodrow Wilson*

EXPANSION C

Describe each of the following people with a sentence that includes one of the idioms from this unit. For most of the people, several answers are possible.

Dick wonders how people can look up a word in the dictionary if they don't know how to spell the word.

Dick is playing with half a deck.

1. Diane will probably be president of the company some day.

   _____

2. Don had more job offers than anyone else in the class when he graduated.

   _____

3. Harry can't decide whether he wants to get married or not. One day he says yes and the next day he says no.

   _____

4. Nick is trying to figure out what to buy his mother for her birthday.

   _____

5. Jane is interested in journalism, so she went to see the editor of a local newspaper to find out more about the field.

   _____

6. Jay went for three days with one of the lenses missing from his glasses and he didn't notice anything wrong.

   _____

7. Ruth published a scholarly paper on her latest scientific discoveries.

   _____

8. When Brad's teacher asked him what the capital of Portugal is, he said it was Madrid.

   _____

9. Terry got a notice from his bank stating that his checking account had insufficient funds, so he wrote out a check to himself and deposited it.

   _____

EXPANSION D

Refer to the events in the Situation at the beginning of this unit to complete the following activities. Use idioms from this unit in your answers.

1. Imagine that you are Sally. Write a letter to your parents and mention the news of your professor.

2. Imagine that you are Bob. It is later the same day and you have just left the class taught by the professor who is **playing with half a deck**. The professor did something stupid again today in class. Tell your roommate about it and then tell him about Dr. Rosenfield.

3. Imagine that you are one of Sally's parents. You have just received a copy of her grades for the semester. Sally made the Dean's list, which means that her grades are among the best. Compose a congratulatory telegram to send her.

4. Imagine that you are Bob. Write a letter to your parents complaining about your professor and comparing him to Dr. Rosenfield.

EXPANSION E   Use idioms from this unit to complete the following roleplays.

1. Work with a classmate to complete this roleplay, which takes place in a school dormitory. Both of you are students who are on the school debate team. Decide which one of you is Student A and which is Student B. Then read only the paragraph that is for your part.

   Student A: A classmate, Bill Bowen, is interested in joining the debate team. You don't know much about him except for the following story. Last year, Bill got a notice from his bank stating that he had overdrawn his account by $25. Bill sent a check for $25 to the bank, but the check was drawn from the same account! You are opposed to Bill's membership on the debate team because you believe Bill is stupid. You are discussing Bill with Student B, another member of the debate team.

   Student B: A classmate, Bill Bowen, is interested in joining the debate team. You don't know Bill personally, but you support his membership because you heard the following story about him. Last year, Bill was stopped by the police for speeding. The police officer is known to students as someone who is very strict. Bill was able to persuade the officer into giving him a warning instead of a ticket. You are discussing Bill with Student A, another member of the debate team.

2. Work with a classmate to complete this roleplay. Both of you work as secretaries in a business office. Decide which one of you is Secretary A and which is Secretary B. Then read only the paragraph that is for your part.

   Secretary A: You have been working in this office for over a year. You really like the company and you really need the money, but you think your boss doesn't know whether she is coming or going. Secretary B has just been hired. You are talking to him/her about the job. You offer to answer any questions he/she may have.

   Secretary B: You have just started your job today. In the same office is Secretary A, who has been there for a year. He/she seems very nice and you would like to be friends. You have lots of questions to ask about the job.

COMMUNICATION   Read and discuss the following.

1. Students have to **put on their thinking caps** when they take exams. Teachers have to **put on their thinking caps** when they prepare lessons. Tell about times when you have to **put on your thinking cap**.

2. If a person **is out in left field**, it means that the person does not know what is happening around him or her. This expression comes from the game of baseball. The player whose position is in left field is far from most of the action in the game. Try to guess what the original meanings of these expressions are:

   be out to lunch   **have a screw loose**

3. People can grow intellectually by getting an education or by undergoing training. A certain type of intellectual competence, however, is known as *common sense*. People are said to have common sense when they are able to make sound practical judgments that are not based upon a formal education or training. Someone who **doesn't know enough to come in out of the rain** is someone who lacks common sense. Give examples of certain types of knowledge that are considered to be common sense.

4. One of the standards that Sally and Bob use in judging their professors is intellectual competence. How important is this standard to you? What other standards do you use in judging the abilities and effectiveness of your professors, as well as others in positions of responsibility?

5. People who do **not know whether they are coming or going** have trouble making decisions. An example of this is a student who changes majors from one semester to the next; in one year this person goes from economics to political science to art. Tell about a time when you (or someone you know) did **not know whether you were coming or going**.

6. Choose one of the following quotations, or choose one that appeared earlier in the unit. Explain its meaning, or think of a situation that illustrates it.

> *We only think when we are confronted with a problem.*
>
> *John Dewey*

> *Many highly intelligent people are poor thinkers. Many people of average intelligence are skilled thinkers. The power of a car is separate from the way the car is driven.*
>
> *Edward de Bono*

130   UNIT 17

Dependability 18

do one's part   pass the buck

count on someone   count someone out

get out of doing something

hold up one's end of the bargain

leave someone high and dry

let someone down

pull one's own weight

shoulder the responsibility

turn one's back on someone

worm out of something

WARM-UP

We live in a world where people depend on each other for help or support. Children, for example, depend on their parents for food and shelter. Complete the following statements, and then compare them with those of your classmates.

Homeowners depend on fire fighters for _____ .

Patients rely on their _____ for diagnoses and treatment.

City dwellers depend on _____ for food.

_____ depend on customers for business.

Students rely on _____ for _____ .

Anita Cooper was recently elected president of a charitable organization that serves her local hospital. One of her duties is to find and train volunteers who will work as nurse's aids. In many hospitals, these volunteers are called *candy stripers* because their red and white uniforms resemble candy canes. Several weeks after taking office, Anita discovered that the candy striper program was a mess. In order to straighten things out, she will have to spend a lot more time at the hospital than she originally thought.

Anita has just returned home from a long day at the hospital. She notices the light blinking on her telephone answering machine. When she pushes the button, she hears the following messages from her daughter, Felicia:

Felicia: Hi, mom. It's just me. It's five o'clock. Call me when you get in. I need to talk to you about something. Bye.

Felicia: Mom, it's me again. It's now a little after seven. I guess you're still at the hospital. I need to talk to you tonight about maybe taking Tommy tomorrow if you can manage it. I just found out today that I have to be out of town on business. The regular sitter can't do it, so I'm really **counting on you**. Talk to you soon. Bye, now.

Anita looked at her calendar and saw that she had scheduled training sessions for the whole next day. She picked up the phone and dialed her daughter's number. She would have to say no. She knew that Felicia would feel she was **letting her down**, but she felt she had no choice.

ANALYSIS & EXPLANATION

Circle the best answer to the question below. Then turn to the appendix, where each answer is explained. If your choice is incorrect, choose again.

Why did Anita feel she had no choice?

A. She knew that her daughter needed her more than the hospital.
B. She didn't like the idea that her daughter depended on her so much.
C. She had made a commitment to the hospital to do the training sessions.

ATTITUDE

Anita feels that when someone makes a commitment, it should be honored because others are depending on that person.

EXPANSION A

Read each of the following situations and decide whether it describes Boris or Gustave. Write *B* for Boris or *G* for Gustave.

Katrina and her younger brothers, Boris and Gustave, are living with their elderly grandmother in a small house in the suburbs. Grandmother depends on Katrina to help out. Katrina, in turn, depends on her brothers. She can generally **count on** Boris, but unfortunately, Gustave isn't very dependable.

_G_ Knowing that Katrina's plane would get in very late at night, he agreed to pick her up at the airport. Her plane arrived on time at 2:00 a.m. Katrina waited and waited, but he never showed up. Public transportation stopped at 1:30, and there were no cabs. He **left Katrina high and dry**.

_____ 1. He agreed to help Katrina paint the kitchen. Katrina bought the paint and the brushes and then said she was ready to start. He claimed that he wasn't feeling well and that the smell of paint made him nauseous. He **wormed out of** helping Katrina.

_____ 2. The next day it snowed. He and Katrina had agreed that they would each shovel half of the driveway every time it snowed. He found the shovels in the basement and got to work right away. He **held up his end of the bargain**.

_____ 3. Katrina **counted on him** to help her mow the lawn and plant the garden in the summer. He would mow the lawn one week, and she would mow it the next week. They also took turns weeding the garden.

_____ 4. One day, Katrina came home to find that the power had been shut off. When she called the electric company, they said the bill had not been paid for three months. He promised to pay the bill the next day. Katrina spent that evening with friends, since she didn't want to sit at home in the dark. When she got home the next day, the electricity still wasn't on. She told him that he **had let her down**.

LEAVE SOMEONE HIGH AND DRY

_____ 5. The three siblings decided to spend one Saturday cleaning the house thoroughly. He agreed to **pull his weight** and clean the kitchen and the bathroom. At the end of the day the rooms were spotless, and Katrina was very pleased.

_____ 6. On that same Saturday, he agreed to vacuum and dust the living room and dining room. Late in the afternoon, he told Katrina that he had hurt his back lifting boxes that morning, so he couldn't possibly clean. Because of his injury, he **got out of** cleaning the two rooms.

_____ 7. Monday night, Katrina did the grocery shopping. When she got home, she asked her brother to help her carry in the groceries. He said to **count him out** because his back was still hurting.

_____ 8. Disgusted, she asked her other brother to help carry in the bags, and he readily agreed to **do his part**.

_____ 9. When Katrina got in her car to go to work Thursday morning, she saw that she was out of gas. She had lent him the car the night before. When she asked him why he hadn't filled up the tank, he **passed the buck** and said he didn't know that he was supposed to.

_____ 10. Katrina decided to change jobs. She took a job that required a lot of travel, so she could no longer accept responsibility for the running of the house. She asked her brothers to take charge of the affairs of the house while she was away. He said he was far too busy and **turned his back on her**.

_____ 11. By contrast, he said he would **shoulder the responsibility** and that she should not worry about the house while she was away.

For each of the following situations, put a plus sign (+) if you think you are being dependable or a minus sign (-) if you think you are being undependable.

_____ Your friend Roberto has moved into a new apartment, and you have agreed to go shopping with him for household supplies. The person you are dating calls and asks you to come over and watch TV. You don't want to **let Roberto down,** but you would rather be with the person you are dating. You call Roberto and tell him you're sick and can't go.

_____ 1. You and your sister are supposed to do the dishes after dinner every night. Last night after dinner your parents went to a meeting, and your sister went to the movies. You decided to read a book. When your parents got home at 10:00 p.m., the dishes were still not done. You **passed the buck** and said it was your sister's fault because she didn't stay home to help you.

_____ 2. Your English class wants to have a party. Your teacher agrees and asks for volunteers to help organize it. Several students step forward, and you decide to **do your part** and volunteer also.

_____ 3. Your sister, who is a single parent, became ill and was rushed to the hospital. Her two small children need someone to take care of them while she is recuperating. You **shoulder the responsibility** and bring them home with you.

_____ 4. You promised your little brother that you would take him to the early show at the movies Saturday night. A friend of yours calls and asks you to a party. You want to go to the party, so you **worm out of** taking your brother to the movies by telling him that the show he wanted to see doesn't start until after his bedtime.

_____ 5. The hospital in your hometown is running out of blood. A committee has been formed to organize a blood drive. On Saturday afternoon volunteers will go to each house and ask residents to donate blood. You agree to **pull your weight** and visit the houses on your street.

_____ 6. Your daughter is on a baseball team for children between the ages of 8 and 12. She is pitching this Wednesday evening and is **counting on you** to be there. You have a previous engagement but make arrangements to reschedule it. You show up at the game.

_____ 7. You live in the city, and your neighborhood is sponsoring a clean-up day. You agree to supply the rakes, brooms, and any other tools that will be needed. The day before the clean-up you have the opportunity to fly to Florida for a week, and you go. You **leave the neighborhood organization high and dry** because it's too late for them to find someone else to supply the tools.

_____ 8. The doorbell rings. It is your next door neighbor. She is very worried about her son who has taken ill and asks you to drive them to the doctor's. You were just about to leave for the airport to catch a plane, but you cannot **turn your back on your neighbor**. You call the airline and change your reservations for later that day.

_____ 9. At a local meeting, everyone on your street agrees to recycle newspapers, which means that once a week someone has to collect all of the newspapers and take them to the recycling center. You **hold up your end of the bargain** and agree to collect and deliver the newspapers the first Saturday of every month.

_____ 10. You belong to a bicycle club. The members are organizing a 40-mile bike ride over the weekend. The president calls you up to see if you will help organize it, but you say to **count you out** because you are recovering from a broken arm and won't be able to participate.

_____ 11. You also belong to a tennis club. Although you didn't really want to, you agreed to teach tennis to elementary school children on Saturday mornings. Although you still could teach the children, you **get out of it** because of your broken arm.

EXPANSION C

You may want to reread the Situation at the beginning of this unit before completing the following activities. Use idioms from this unit in your answers.

1. Suppose you are Anita and you return the call to Felicia. This time, however, it is you who must leave a message on your daughter's machine. Write down two versions of what you might say. In the first version, you break the news to her gently. In the second version, you are very direct.

2. Suppose you are Felicia. You have no one to look after Tommy, so you write a memo to your boss in which you try to **get out of** the work assignment that takes you out of town.

EXPANSION D

Write five statements about unusual or interesting things that you have done or that have happened to you. Three or more of the statements must be true, but one or two can be false. When you finish writing your statements, tell them to your classmates and see if they can guess which of your statements are false. Include one idiom from this unit in each of your statements.

_____

_____

_____

_____

_____

1. Traditional marriage vows in the United States place great value on dependability. At a wedding ceremeony, both the bride and the groom are asked to promise that they will love each other "for better or for worse, in sickness and in health," meaning that they will be able to rely on each other in good times and in bad times. Do marriage vows in your country have a similar emphasis?

2. Tell a classmate about a time when someone **left you high and dry**, but don't say what you did in response. Ask your classmate what he or she would have done in the same situation, and then say what you did.

3. Harry S. Truman, president of the United States from 1945–1953, had a sign on his desk in the Oval Office of the White House that read, "The buck stops here." Using your knowledge of the expression **pass the buck**, explain what this message meant.

4. The expression **leave someone high and dry** is derived from the action of taking a ship out of water for storage, maintenance, or repairs. How is a person like a ship in this expression?

5. Think of an unpleasant job or task. Describe the task to several classmates and ask them how they might **worm out of doing it** diplomatically.

Problem Solving
19

be off base   hem and haw

miss the mark   skirt the issue

be right on target

beat around the bush

get down to brass tacks

get to the heart of something

hit the bull's eye

hit the nail on the head

take the bull by the horns

zero in on something

WARM-UP

Suppose you are writing a letter of recommendation for someone and you want to comment on that person's excellent performance in solving problems. Add to the list of expressions below that might be used in writing your recommendation.

solves problems before they become critical

highly decisive in dealing with difficult problems

uses a variety of analytical techniques to solve problems

The mayor of a large city in the United States formed a special commission to solve the city's trash problem. The city had always disposed of its trash by dumping millions of tons of it every year into huge holes in the ground. In recent years, however, the number of dumps has decreased significantly, and the cost of finding new sites has gone up a great deal.

After months of considering solutions that would be economically attractive and environmentally safe, the commission compiled a lengthy report that makes several very specific recommendations. The mayor has read the report, and she is meeting with the head of the commission. Their meeting is about to end.

Mayor Sanchez:	Well, all in all, I think we can accept most of your recommendations, Stan. No question about it: you've **hit the nail on the head** when you say we are producing far too much trash. Your figures are impressive—and scary. I had some idea, of course, of the magnitude of the problem, but I didn't think it was this bad.
Stan:	And it's getting worse every year. That's why we urge you to begin a recycling program as soon as possible.
Mayor Sanchez:	Your other recommendation to build a trash-to-steam plant will probably be hard to sell to City Council, but if you do as good a job convincing them as you did with me, then we'll be OK. Just go in there on Monday and **take the bull by the horns**.
Secretary:	I'm sorry to interrupt, Mayor, but you're behind schedule.
Mayor Sanchez:	What am I doing next?
Secretary:	Television interview.
Mayor Sanchez:	Can't keep the press waiting, can I? Good luck on Monday, Stan.

ANALYSIS & EXPLANATION

Circle the best answer to the question below. Then turn to the appendix, where each answer is explained. If your choice is incorrect, choose again.

Why does the mayor decide to accept the recommendations of the report?

A. She thinks the recommendations of the commission are affordable.

B. She thinks the commission did a good job in identifying practical solutions.

C. She thinks the problem needs an immediate solution.

ATTITUDE

The mayor admires the ability to identify and explain solutions to problems.

EXPANSION A

Answer the question at the end of each of the situations below with *yes* or *no*.

yes   Randy spends every penny he earns. He knows this isn't wise, so he's decided to **take the bull by the horns** and figure out a way to save some money. In other words, Randy will have to take direct action to solve his problem even though it may be difficult. Do you think Randy is going to try and change his spending habits?

_____   1. The next day, Randy got out his financial records and started to **zero in on** all unnecessary purchases. In other words, he concentrated on identifying things he bought that he didn't need. Do you think Randy is making any progress on solving his problem?

_____   2. Next, Randy looked at how much of his paycheck went toward rent. The maximum he should pay is between 25% and 33% of his salary. Randy is paying 40%. At last, he felt he was **getting to the heart of** the problem. In other words, Randy thought he was beginning to understand one of the most important parts of the problem. Do you think perhaps Randy should consider moving to a cheaper apartment?

_____   3. Randy suspected he spent far too much money on food, but his calculations showed that only about 8% of his paycheck went to groceries. Rather than **hitting the nail on the head**, Randy **was off base** in thinking that too much money was going for groceries. In other words, he thought he was right, but he was wrong. Do you think Randy should spend less money on food?

_____   4. Next Randy looked at how much he spent on clothes. He thought he could save money by cutting back a great deal in this area. Much to his surprise, however, he discovered that he hadn't bought any new clothes for over six months. He really **missed the mark** on this one. In other words, he was wrong. Do you think Randy will be able to save money by spending less on clothes?

TAKE THE BULL BY THE HORNS

_____ 5. As Randy was working, the telephone rang. It was his sister, Jill. As they talked, Randy told her about his financial problems and asked if she had any suggestions. She immediately **got down to brass tacks**. In other words, she identified the basic or essential parts of the problem. Do you think Jill was trying to be helpful?

_____ 6. Jill told Randy that one of her biggest expenses was her electric bill. She knew that Randy had several air conditioning units and that they are very expensive to operate. Randy checked his electric bills and agreed that he was paying too much. Jill's analysis **was right on target.** In other words, she was correct in identifying the source of one of Randy's problems. Do you think Randy will be more careful about using his air conditioners?

_____ 7. Jill pointed out that Randy's financial problems would disappear if he had more money. Randy didn't say much in reply. He just **hemmed and hawed**. She wondered if he considered asking for a raise. Randy **beat around the bush**. Then she asked him if he thought about looking for a job that paid more. He **skirted the issue**. In other words, he wouldn't give her a direct answer to her questions. Do you think Randy wanted to talk to Jill about this subject?

_____ 8. When Randy hung up, he remembered one more category—the telephone. He got out his phone bills and looked at them. He noticed he made a lot of long distance calls every month. He found another area he could economize on. He **hit the bull's eye**. In other words, he was correct in identifying one reason for his financial problems. Do you think Randy will be making as many long distance calls in the future?

EXPANSION B

Read the passage below. Then respond to the statements that follow it; write _A_ for Agree or _D_ for Disagree.

On Monday night, Stan Gentry and the other members of the commission presented their report to City Council. First, they discussed the problem in a very general way, but soon they **got down to brass tacks**. The reaction was very mixed. Council President Braxton urged the Council to **take the bull by the horns** and vote for the recommendations because he thought they **were right on target**. So did Councilwoman Lopez who said she thought the report really **got to the heart of** the problem. Councilman Silver concurred, saying that the report **hit the bull's eye**. However, Councilwoman Richter thought that one recommendation in particular **was** completely **off base**. She **zeroed in on** the trash-to-steam plant, which she thought the city could not afford to build. When she challenged Gentry about his estimated construction costs, he **skirted the issue**. When she repeated her questions, he continued to **beat around the bush**. Finally, Richter told him to stop **hemming and hawing** and give her some direct answers. Under pressure, he admitted that he might have **missed the mark** in estimating the construction costs. Richter moved that Council study the trash-to-steam recommendation more, but she favored the recommendation to recycle, saying that it **hit the nail on the head**. Councilwoman Richter's motion passed unanimously.

_A_   Council members Braxton, Lopez, and Silver originally supported the recommendations of the report because they believed that the commission had done an excellent job in identifying the problem and proposing solutions.

_____ 1. It was Councilwoman Richter who thought that some of the conclusions of the report were faulty.

_____ 2. Richter focused on the recommendation to build the trash-to-steam plant because she thought it was probably too expensive.

_____ 3. Gentry avoided Richter's questions about construction costs because he hadn't researched the answers to them.

_____ 4. Richter finally was able to get Gentry to admit that his original estimates were probably wrong.

_____ 5. Richter supported the recommendation to begin a program of recycling, and she was able to convince everyone else on Council to delay voting on the trash-to-steam solution.

EXPANSION C

Read the problem below. Then write three solutions to it, each on a separate piece of paper. One statement should be a solution that hits the nail on the head, one should be off base, and one should skirt the issue. When you are finished, put all of the pieces of paper together and read them aloud. After reading each one, discuss it using idioms from this unit.

Experts project that the human population of Earth will double to over ten billion in the twenty-first century, with 90% of the increase occurring in poorer countries. In the poorest countries today, the growth in population is already exceeding the ability of those nations to provide housing, food, and fuel to their citizenry. What do you think can be done by governments and international organizations to help in solving this problem?

EXPANSION D   Read and do the following activity.

1. Together as a class, take five minutes to make a list of several specific problems that students in your school are experiencing or that people in your community are having. Do this now before you read the next instruction.

2. Divide into groups. Each group should have four (or more) members. Do this now before you read the next instruction.

3. Each group should choose one of the problems from the list that you made in the first step. Do this now before you read the next instruction.

4. Divide each group into two subgroups. Subgroup A should read instruction 5a ONLY, and Subgroup B should read instruction 5b ONLY. Do this now.

5a. You and the others in Subgroup A have ten minutes to **take the bull by the horns** and **get to the heart of** the problem that your group has selected. At the end of this time, you will propose your solutions to Subgroup B and pressure them into accepting your solutions.

5b. In ten minutes, Subgroup A will present solutions to the problem your group has selected. They will want you to accept their solutions. You and the others in Subgroup B, however, are going to do everything you can to **skirt the issue, beat around the bush,** and **hem and haw**. While Subgroup A is preparing, you should try to guess the solutions they might propose.

> *The effective worker is one who turns problems into opportunities.*
>
> *Anonymous*

1. A successful doctor is one who is able to **zero in on** a patient's illness. Often, however, a successful lawyer is one who is able to **beat around the bush** in defending a client. Below is a list of other occupations. Separate them into those whose jobs require them to **zero in on** a problem and those whose jobs require them to **beat around the bush**. Support your answers.

detective	public relations officer
politician	army general
teacher	diplomat
scientist	air traffic controller

2. *Darts* is a game in which small slender arrows are thrown at a target. The target is divided into several concentric circles, at the center of which is a small circle, usually black, called a *bull's eye*. It is very difficult of course for a dart to **hit the bull's eye**. This idiom can be reduced to an informal expression that is used when a desired result is achieved. If, for example, someone asks you a question and you give an answer that is precisely to the point, your questioner might simply say, "Bull's eye!" Write several exchanges that end with one person saying, "Bull's eye!"

_____

_____

_____

_____

3. What is the difference between solving problems and solving the symptoms of problems? Which one **gets to the heart of** the matter? Can you give an example of each?

4. Think of examples in history when people thought they **were right on target** but later learned that they **were way off base**. For example, people once thought that the sun revolved around the earth, but later they learned that the opposite occurs.

5. One day when Harry Truman was President of the United States, he called in his top economic adviser, Edwin Nourse, for a meeting. Nourse kept **hemming and hawing** in response to Truman's questions: "On the one hand, yes, Mr. President. On the other hand, no." Truman turned to an aide and asked, "Do you think you can find me a one-armed economist?" What did President Truman mean by this remark? What message was he sending to Nourse?

6. Choose one of the following quotations, or choose the saying on p. 143. Explain its meaning, or think of a situation that illustrates it.

> *The best way out is always through.*
> **Robert Frost**

> *Most people spend more time and energy in going around problems than in trying to solve them.*
> **Henry Ford**

Individual **20** Achievement

get ahead   be top dog

make it big   outdo oneself

bring up the rear   come a long way

be the cream of the crop

come in first/second/third/last

feather in one's cap

make it to the top

make something out of oneself

not hold a candle to someone

place first/second/third

play second fiddle to someone

WARM-UP

In many senior high schools in the United States, students in the graduating class vote for classmates who excel in different areas such as talent, good looks, friendliness, and athletic ability. One especially important category is the person who is most likely to succeed in life. Write down who in your class is the most likely to succeed, and give a reason for your vote. Then read your choice to your classmates.

_____

_____

_____

Every year, high schools around the United States hold spelling contests. Winners from each school compete against each other until a small number of finalists are named. The finalists go to Washington, D.C., to the National Spelling Bee Championship. Earlier today, George won in a competition held at his high school. One of George's classmates is Mary, who is also a friend and neighbor of his. Mary has just come home from school. Her mother is in the kitchen making a sandwich.

Mother: Mary? Is that you?

Mary: Hi, I'm home!

Mother: Hi, honey. Anything exciting to report today?

Mary: The big news is that George won. He actually **came in first** in the spelling bee today.

Mother: Well, that's quite an achievement, and he should be proud of himself. So, what was the winning word?

Mary: Mayonnaise. Can you believe it? I guess it's a lot harder to spell than you think.

Mother: M-A-Y-O-N.... Is it one "n" or two?

Mary: See what I mean?

Mother: You know, I can remember when George's parents and his teachers were real worried about his spelling. That was just a couple of years ago. He sure **has come a long way**. So, what happens next?

Mary: There is a play-off against the winner from Central High next week, and then the districts, and after that the state. Who knows, maybe we'll be neighbors to the next national champ.

Mother: Maybe. Speaking of mayonnaise, could you get me the jar from the fridge?

Mary: Only if you can spell it correctly.

INDIVIDUAL ACHIEVEMENT ⟨**147**⟩

Circle the best answer to the question below. Then turn to the appendix, where each answer is explained. If your choice is incorrect, choose again.

What does Mary's mother think of the news about George?

A. She thinks he deserves recognition for his achievement because even she can't spell mayonnaise.

B. She is surprised that he won because he was such a poor speller a few years ago.

C. She is happy about George's achievement, especially because it came after much effort.

ATTITUDE

Mary and her mother admire achievement that comes about through special effort or superior ability, and they believe that such achievement should be publicly recognized.

EXPANSION A

Read each of the following situations. Then respond to the last statement in each situation; write A for Agree or D for Disagree.

___D___ Barb coaches women's hockey, and this year her team made it all the way to the state play-offs, where they **came in second**. Barb and her team probably aren't disappointed.

_____ 1. Peggy can play very complicated pieces on the piano. Martha is just beginning to learn and can only play very simple pieces. When it comes to playing the piano, Martha **doesn't hold a candle to** Peggy. Peggy probably makes lots of mistakes.

_____ 2. Lisa was accepted at one of the best universities in the country. Only a small number of applicants are admitted every year. Lisa **is** among **the cream of the crop**. Lisa probably had very good grades in high school.

_____ 3. Both Larry and Sue are excellent newspaper reporters, but Larry has been with the paper much longer than Sue so he always gets the best assignments. Sue has to **play second fiddle to** Larry. Probably not as many people read Sue's stories as read Larry's.

_____ 4. John and Sally invited some friends over for dinner one night. They spent the whole day preparing the food. They usually just throw something in the microwave, but this time they really **outdid themselves**. John and Sally's friends are probably going to be surprised.

_____ 5. In the last twenty years, Sandy has worked as a teacher's aide, a teacher, a guidance counselor, and a school principal. Today, she is school superintendent. She sure **has come a long way** in twenty years. Sandy probably knows very little about running schools.

_____ 6. Andy is a salesperson for a medical supply company. Yesterday, he signed an exclusive contract with a chain of hospitals. Getting such a big contract really was a **feather in his cap**. Andy probably can't wait to tell his boss the news.

BE TOP DOG

_____ 7. Jill was on one of those TV game shows where contestants win cash and prizes by answering questions correctly. Jill **placed first** by answering the question, "What is the second largest city in Togo?" Jill probably also knows what the largest city in Togo is.

_____ 8. Carla worked as an office assistant for several years, but the position didn't pay much. In order to **get ahead**, Carla enrolled in evening classes at a local college. After finishing them, Carla was promoted to office administrator. Carla probably is making more money now.

_____ 9. As a student, Margaret was average. No one really expected her to be particularly successful in life. However, today she is president and owner of one of the most successful advertising firms in the state. Margaret certainly has **made something out of herself**. Her teachers probably aren't surprised.

_____ 10. The football team at Wanamaker College is at the end of the season and it has a perfect record: 0 wins and 9 losses. This is the third year in a row that Wanamaker has placed last. Once again, Wanamaker is **bringing up the rear**. The coach probably should be worried.

_____ 11. Steve just got a small part on a television show. His director told him that he has exceptional talent and if he applies himself, maybe he'll **make it big** some day. Steve probably will start looking for another career after hearing that.

_____ 12. Six months ago, no one had heard of Michele Stevens. But then she published a novel that became the number one best-seller. Michele **made it to the top** overnight. Her life probably has changed a lot.

_____ 13. It took Ann fifteen years of hard work, but her efforts finally paid off. Yesterday, she was promoted to manager. She**'s top dog** in her division now. Ann probably moved to a new office.

Read the passage below. Then respond to the statements that follow it; write *A* for Agree or *D* for Disagree.

Jill is a swimmer—a very good swimmer. In fact, no one can **hold a candle to** her when it comes to the 800-meter freestyle. She always **places first** in that event, and last week she really **outdid herself** by setting a new world record. She beat the old record by more than a second, putting quite a **feather in her cap**. Jill also does very well in the 400-meter freestyle, usually **coming in first or second**. Very few people were surprised to hear that she was named to the U.S. Olympic Team. Jill finally **made it to the top**. At the next games, she'll have a chance to compete against the **cream of the crop** from many other countries.

Getting to **be top dog** is seldom easy for anyone, and Jill is no exception. She wasn't allowed to compete during the first year she was on her high school team. The coach made her **play second fiddle to** her teammates because they were older and had more experience. Finally, in one *meet* (an athletic competition), the coach had to use her because one of the other swimmers got injured. In her heart, Jill knew she could win, but she was so nervous that she **came in last**. The memory of her **bringing up the rear** that day was impossible for her to forget. In fact, she even had nightmares about it. Jill knew that if she ever was going to **make something of herself** as a swimmer, she would have to learn to control her nervousness. Her fear of competing in public was the only thing that kept her from **getting ahead**. It took more than a few sessions with the school psychologist, but eventually Jill regained her confidence and conquered her fear. Since then, she has spent most of her life in a swimming pool.

Jill certainly has **come a long way.** She **made it big** at an early age, and there is every reason to think she will **make it even bigger** in the future.

_____ 1. Jill is probably under 25.

_____ 2. Jill generally does better in swimming events that involve shorter distances.

_____ 3. Some people were surprised to hear that Jill will go to the next Olympics.

_____ 4. Jill's high school coach recognized and encouraged her talent from the start.

_____ 5. Jill was nervous the first time she competed because she was afraid of getting injured.

_____ 6. Many times, Jill relived the day she lost the swimming meet.

_____ 7. Jill overcame her fear of losing without help from anyone.

_____ 8. Jill probably has a bright future.

EXPANSION C

Use an idiom to describe the people in each of the following situations. There may be more than one acceptable idiom for each.

Mary entered a race. She crossed the finish line in a little over three minutes. Only one person finished before her, with a time of two minutes and fifty-seven seconds.

Mary placed second in the race. OR *Mary came in second.*

1. Angela spent days researching and then writing a paper for one of her classes. She was sure this paper was the best one she had ever written.

2. Brian is one of three purchasers for a chain of department stores. Last year and again this year, the store sold more of what the other purchasers bought than of what Brian bought.

3. Ann sent a memo to her boss that identified several ways the company could save quite a bit of money by making some changes in procedures. Her boss not only agreed to the recommendations, but also recommended a salary increase for Ann.

4. Joann started her own company many years ago. Since then, it has grown from three employees in one small office to three hundred in a ten-story building.

5. People always compare Bill to Jim. Both are terrific tennis players, but the coach seldom lets Bill play because Jim is a senior and Bill is only a sophomore. When Jim graduates, all that will change.

6. Terri first ran for office ten years ago. She wanted to be on the city council, but she lost. Two years later, she ran again and won. Five years ago, she successfully ran for mayor. This year, she won the race for a seat in the U.S. Senate.

7. Jim works as a bagger in a grocery store. After three years of putting groceries in bags for customers, he's grown bored. He would like to be a cashier, but he's not qualified. He decided to take a training course.

8. Al challenged Ken to a game of chess. Ken has played for years and is very good. Al has only been playing for a short time, but he isn't bad. It is very unlikely, however, that Al will win.

9. Bob's soccer team has won most of their games this season. They have been invited to compete in a national competition. All the teams that have been invited are among the best in the country.

_____

10. Alice is an experienced computer programmer. Sue has just started working at the same job, so she isn't nearly as good as Alice.

_____

EXPANSION D

Refer to the events in the Situation at the beginning of this unit to do the following activities. Use idioms from this unit in your answers.

1. Imagine that you are a student contestant in a spelling competition. What might you say to a contestant before you start if that person is someone of the opposite sex? Someone of the same sex? A close friend? Someone you don't know?

2. What might you say at the end if you win? If you lose?

3. Imagine that you are the school principal. Your role is to say a few words to both contestants at the end of the competition. What might you say to George, the champion, and to Ellen, the student who **came in second**?

4. Now imagine that you are one of Ellen's parents. You were present at the competition. What might you say to Ellen?

5. Imagine that you are George's English teacher. You are proud of the progress George has made over the years in improving his spelling, and you are especially proud of his achievement today. What might you say to him when you see him?

6. Imagine you are George. It is later the same day. You are home now in your room. You open your diary and are about to write down the day's events and what you thought of them. Your thoughts are also on the future and how your life might be affected if you make it to the National Championship in Washington.

> *Nothing great was ever achieved without enthusiasm.*
>
> *Ralph Waldo Emerson*

COMMUNICATION   Read and discuss the following.

1. Everyone is able to do at least one thing well, so use your imagination to think of an achievement award for each of your classmates. For example, a classmate who goes to films and talks about them a lot can be given the "best film critic" award. Present your awards in front of the class.

2. It is sometimes said that *life at the top is lonely.* What do you suppose is meant by this expression?

3. In many societies, awards or prizes are given to outstanding achievers. Internationally, perhaps the best known awards are the Nobel Prizes, given for accomplishments in physics, chemistry, medicine-physiology, literature, and peace. In the United States, Pulitzer Prizes are awarded for achievements in journalism, literature, drama, and music. The Motion Picture Academy recognizes achievement in the film industry by giving "Oscars." The National Academy of Recording Arts & Sciences gives "Grammies." In sports, athletes are given awards for being the "Most Valuable Player." If achievement in your society is publicly recognized, what forms does it take? If it isn't, can you explain why not?

4. Choose one of the following quotations, or choose the one on p. 152. Explain its meaning, or think of a situation that illustrates it.

> *It is a sobering thought, that when Mozart was my age, he had been dead for two years.*
>
> *Tom Lehrer*

> *When your work speaks for itself, don't interrupt.*
>
> *Henry Kaiser*

> *Anyone can sympathize with the sufferings of a friend, but it requires a very fine nature to sympathize with a friend's success.*
>
> *Oscar Wilde*

Speed

21

in a flash   *step on it*

get moving   *make tracks*

drag one's feet   *get a move on*

at a snail's pace

get the ball rolling

get the show on the road

in no time (flat)

like a bat out of hell

set a world record

take one's (good old) time

WARM-UP

Many kinds of workers are expected to perform certain duties at high levels of speed. A secretary, for example, can be required to take dictation or type a particular number of words per minute. Think of several occupations and duties associated with them that involve speed.

_____

_____

_____

_____

Pam Carpenter works from nine to five, five days a week. She often uses her half-hour lunch break to run errands. Today, she has several stops to make. Her first one is the pharmacy.

Pharmacist: Who's next, please?
Pam: I believe I am.
Pharmacist: *(looking at the prescription)* OK. This shouldn't be a problem. Why don't you take a seat?
Pam: I can come back if you think it'll take a while.
Pharmacist: Well, that's up to you, but I shouldn't be more than a few minutes.
Pam: Oh? It usually takes a lot longer than that.
Pharmacist: At this pharmacy?
Pam: Well, no. Actually, this is my first time here.
Pharmacist: Yeah. I don't remember seeing you before. Well, I'll be back **in no time**.

True to his word, the pharmacist returned in a few minutes with Pam's medicine. As he rang up her purchase on the cash register, Pam said:

Pam: Well, that *was* fast. In fact, I think you just **set a world record**!
Pharmacist: Thanks. We aim to please!

ANALYSIS & EXPLANATION

Circle the best answer to the question below. Then turn to the appendix, where each answer is explained. If your choice is incorrect, choose again.

Why did Pam appreciate the service she received at the pharmacy?

A. She was running late and needed to get back to the office.
B. The pharmacist provided friendly and courteous service.
C. The pharmacist filled her order quickly.

ATTITUDE

Pam admires the ability of people to take speedy action in an effort to make progress on something.

EXPANSION A

Answer the question at the end of each situation below with *yes* or *no*.

yes   Mary started cooking dinner fifteen minutes ago and it's ready already. She cooked the meal **in a flash**. Did Mary cook the meal fast?

_____   1. Lee has a test in the morning and he needs to spend several hours studying for it. He has been on the phone talking to a friend for the last half hour. Before that, he was watching television. It's now 10:30. Lee had better **get moving** soon. If he doesn't, will he have a tough time on the exam?

_____   2. John left class because he had to feed the parking meter. He said he would be back **in no time flat**. He left a minute ago. Here he comes now. Did he miss much of the lecture?

_____   3. Ann woke up an hour ago, but she doesn't feel like getting out of bed this morning. Her mother told her to **get a move on** or she would be late for school. Was Ann a little slow this morning?

_____   4. Nate rented a ladder for the afternoon so he could make some repairs to his roof. It's already 4:00 and Nate hasn't started working yet. If he doesn't **get the ball rolling** soon, it will be too dark for him to work. Might Nate have to rent the ladder for an additional day?

AT A SNAIL'S PACE

_____ 5. All the cars on the road passed Terry because he was driving **at a snail's pace**. Was Terry driving faster than the law allows?

_____ 6. It took Sally half an hour to do a ten-minute job. She was really **dragging her feet**. Was Sally wasting time?

_____ 7. Eddie was walking down the street when a ferocious looking dog began chasing him. Frightened, Eddie took off **like a bat out of hell**. Did Eddie run as fast as he could to get away?

_____ 8. Bill has invited friends over for dinner at 8:00. The clock has just struck six, and Bill hasn't even gone shopping for food yet. If he doesn't **get the show on the road** soon, his friends will have to eat somewhere else. Is Bill going to have to hurry?

_____ 9. Sandy is good at accounting so she always does her own tax returns every year. Most people spend hours and hours on their taxes. Sandy gets hers done in a fraction of that time. Last year, she was so fast she almost **set a world record**. Does Sandy spend much time doing her taxes?

_____ 10. Margaret was driving to her doctor's office for a two o'clock appointment. Her watch read 1:55. Margaret decided to **step on it** so she wouldn't be late. Did Margaret speed up?

_____ 11. Andy ran an errand for his mother. It always took her about an hour to do it, but Andy didn't come back for three hours! He **took his good old time**. Was Andy in a hurry?

_____ 12. Every Friday night, Kim lets her children watch a video. The rental shop is only open another twenty minutes, so Kim has got to **make tracks** if she wants to get there before it closes. Will Kim hurry?

Read the passage below. Then respond to the statements that follow it; write *A* for Agree or *D* for Disagree.

When Joann heard that her favorite singer, Julio Estevan, was going to give a concert in her area, she ran out and bought two tickets. One ticket was for her and the other was for her husband, Jay. Jay, however, wasn't very excited about going. On the evening of the concert, Joann got ready **in a flash**, but Jay **took his good old time** even though Joann told him to **get a move on** several times. At 7:00, an hour before the concert was to start, Joann told Jay that they had better **get moving**. The drive normally takes thirty minutes, but Joann was sure it would take longer this time because Jay was driving **at a snail's pace**. She asked him to **step on it**, but he didn't speed up much.

A couple of minutes later, Jay noticed that the car was almost out of gas, so he pulled over to a service station. The attendant must have **set a world record** filling up the tank, but he really **dragged his feet** filling out the credit card slip. Worried that they would be late, Joann asked Jay if he minded if she drove. They switched seats and Joann drove **like a bat out of hell** the rest of the way.

Ten minutes later, they pulled into the parking lot. In the lobby, Jay told Joann he needed to visit the men's room before they went to their seats. Joann looked at her watch and reminded Jay that the concert started in five minutes. Jay assured her he would be back **in no time flat**.

They got to their seats at 8:00. Five minutes went by, then ten, then fifteen, but no concert. People were starting to get annoyed. Jay turned to Joann and said, "If they don't **get the show on the road** pretty soon, they're going to have a riot on their hands." Joann, too, began to wonder when they were going to **get the ball rolling**. Finally, one of the organizers of the concert went to the microphone to announce that Julio's plane had landed a short while ago and that Julio was **making tracks** to the concert hall. Several minutes later, Julio appeared on the stage and the audience cheered. About fifteen minutes into the performance, Jay fell asleep.

_A_   Joann probably bought the tickets before discussing it with Jay.

_____ 1. Jay probably was slow in getting dressed for the concert because he couldn't decide what to wear.

_____ 2. They drove to the concert because it probably was too far to walk.

_____ 3. Traffic probably was heavy; this explains why Jay was driving slowly.

_____ 4. The gas station attendant was slow in completing the credit card paperwork because he probably was slow at everything.

_____ 5. Joann probably decided to drive because Jay wouldn't go any faster.

_____ 6. Joann probably passed a lot of cars when she was driving.

_____ 7. There probably were not a lot of people in line ahead of Jay at the men's room.

_____ 8. People probably were beginning to get irritated because they were getting tired of sitting down.

_____ 9. The concert probably ended at the regular time.

_____ 10. This is probably the last time Joann takes Jay to a Julio Estevan concert.

EXPANSION C

Steve's boss, Helen, walked in his office and saw Steve sitting at his desk reading a newspaper. She asked him about the report that he was supposed to have finished but didn't. This is what she told him:

Let's get a move on.

You're going at a snail's pace.

1. Steve realized that things looked bad for him. The truth is that he forgot all about the deadline for the report. He apologized and assured Helen she would have the finished report by the end of the day. This is what he said:

   _____

   _____

2. Helen returned to her office and telephoned her boss to say that the report wasn't ready yet. Her boss, Mark, wasn't at all pleased to hear this because he had planned to take the report with him that afternoon when he left for a business trip. This is what he said to Helen:

   _____

   _____

3. Helen promised Mark he would have the report before he left. As soon as she hung up, she called Steve and explained the situation. She told him to speed things up. This is what she said to him:

   _____

   _____

4. Steve could tell Helen was upset. He told her he was working as fast as he possibly could. This is what he said to Helen:

   _____

   _____

> *This strange disease of modern life, with its sick hurry.*
> **Thomas Carlyle**

> *In skating over thin ice, our safety is in our speed.*
> **Ralph Waldo Emerson**

EXPANSION D Use idioms from this unit to complete the following activities.

1. Work with two other classmates to complete this roleplay, which takes place at someone's home. Two of you are workers, and one of you is the homeowner. Decide which part you will play, and read only the paragraph that describes your role.

   Homeowner: You've agreed to pay two workers by the hour to do some repairs around your house. You think they are **taking their good old time** about getting the job done. Not only do they seem to be working **at a snail's pace**, but they seem to take breaks every half hour. The next time they take a break, you are going to go out there and tell them to **get moving**. And you're not going to accept any excuses.

   Two workers: You and a co-worker have agreed to do some repairs on a house. The owner is paying you by the hour, but the hourly amount is way below average. Even so, you think you are doing a good job. You're working carefully because the work is dangerous. You also are taking a lot of breaks, because the work is tiring.

2. Work with two other classmates to complete this roleplay, which takes place at a school track meet. Two of you are runners, and one of you is a reporter for the school newspaper. Decide which part you will play, and read only the paragraph that describes your role.

   Reporter: Interview both runners at the same time. Runner A was expected to win, but came in last. Runner B surprised everyone by winning. Ask each runner to comment on the other's performance. Runner A will want to leave before your interview is finished, but don't let her/him.

   Runner A: You usually run **like a bat out of hell**, but today was different. You placed last. You are not looking forward to this interview, so at the earliest opportunity you say that you have to **get a move on**.

   Runner B: You usually run **at a snail's pace**, but today was different. You placed first. Runner A has always made fun of your record, so today is your chance to get revenge. Be sure to comment on your excellent performance and also on Runner A's poor performance.

> *Haste makes waste.*
>
> *Anonymous*

> *Now here, you see, it takes all the running you can do, to keep in the same place. If you want to get somewhere else, you must run at least twice as fast as that.*
>
> *Lewis Carroll*

1. When runners begin a race before the starting signal is given, they are said to *jump the gun*. In general, this expression means to "act too hastily." Think of a time when you or someone you know *jumped the gun*.

2. The idiom **step on it** has its origin in something that a driver does to increase the speed at which the vehicle is traveling. What is it that the driver steps on?

3. In sports, a *record* is an account of the performance of an athlete or a team. The idiom *in record time* means the best rate ever recorded. Two other related idioms are *break a record* and **set a world record.** Both can be used with reference to speed, but they are not limited to it. What else can they refer to?

4. A *speed demon* is a person with great energy who travels or works at high speeds. On the road, this behavior is always thought to be negative. In the workplace, however, it might be positive or it might be negative. Think of situations to illustrate both.

5. People can be self-motivated to do something, or they can be motivated by someone else. In the second instance, many of the idioms in this unit can be used.

Let's get moving.	**Let's get the show on the road.**
Get a move on.	**Let's make tracks.**
Let's get the ball rolling.	**Step on it.**

Using one of these idioms may or may not be enough to move someone to action. When it isn't, then some reward or punishment can be attached. This is called the *carrot or stick* approach to getting fast results. Think of a situation in which you or someone you know responded to the "carrot" approach. Now think of a situation in which the "stick" approach was effective.

6. Choose one of the sayings or quotations that appeared earlier in the unit. Explain its meaning, or think of a situation that illustrates it.

22 Composure

fall apart   *calm down*

hold up   *go crazy*

go to pieces   *brace oneself*

be beside oneself

come apart at the seams

fight back the tears

get a hold of oneself

keep a cool head

not blink an eye

pull oneself together

take the news pretty well/badly

WARM-UP

The control that people have of their emotions or reactions is called *composure.* People might lose their composure when they have intense feelings of grief, fear, anger, or even happiness. Ask several of your classmates to tell you about a time when they (or someone they know) lost their composure.

_____

_____

_____

_____

Victor Garcia is an auto mechanic. At work today he was checking the underside of a car when a part dropped on his head and he lost consciousness. Victor's supervisor, Dan, drove him to the hospital where he was admitted to the emergency room for treatment. Dan is telephoning the news to Victor's wife, Ramona.

Ramona: Hello.

Dan: Ramona? It's Dan from the garage.

Ramona: Dan? Victor's not here. Isn't he at work?

Dan: Ramona, I'm calling about Vic. I have something to tell you. **Brace yourself** for some bad news.

Ramona: What do you mean? What's happened?

Dan: Vic was in a little accident this morning, but he's all right now.

Ramona: What? Where is he? Where are you calling from?

Dan: We're at the hospital.

Ramona: What? This can't be.

Dan: Listen to me, Ramona. I said he's all right. *(pause)* Ramona? Ramona, are you still there?

Ramona: I'm OK. I just needed a minute to **pull myself together**. All right. I'm ready now. Tell me what happened.

Victor: Let me put the doctor on. She'll explain everything.

The doctor tells Ramona that Victor had a concussion (an injury to the brain caused by a violent blow), but she won't know how serious it is until the test results come in. Ramona wants to see Victor immediately, but the doctor tells her he can't have any visitors now, so there is no point in her coming to the hospital. She says that she will call again when she knows something. Dan comes back on the line.

Dan: Ramona, I know how you must feel. If there's anything I can do....

Ramona: Thanks, Dan. I have to get off the phone now. The kids will be home from school any minute, and I don't know what to say to them. I need some time to think.

Dan: I understand. I'll call in a few hours. Bye, Ramona.

ANALYSIS & EXPLANATION

Circle the best answer to the question below. Then turn to the appendix, where each answer is explained. If your choice is incorrect, choose again.

How would you describe Ramona's reaction to the news that her husband is in the hospital?

A. She was concerned but not alarmed because Dan assured her that Victor was OK.

B. She was very upset at first, but then she seemed to regain control of herself.

C. She was in a state of emotional shock and was barely able to function.

ATTITUDE

Ramona and Dan think that there are times when it is best for people to show that they are in complete control of their feelings and behavior.

EXPANSION A

Read the passage below. Then answer the questions that follow it with *yes* or *no*.

While some people might **fall apart** in a similar situation, Ramona is very good at **keeping a cool head** in a crisis. She immediately phoned her mother-in-law, who **was beside herself** with worry when she first heard what had happened, but she **got a hold of herself** very quickly. Next, Ramona called Victor's brother, Steven. She thought he might **come apart at the seams**, but he **didn't blink an eye** when she told him. Then she took the phone off the hook so she wouldn't be interrupted when she talked to the children.

She called Robbie into the kitchen and sent the two youngest children upstairs. She was worried that Robbie might **go to pieces**, so she told him to **brace himself** for some bad news. Robbie **took the news** of his father's accident **pretty badly**, but she thought that under the circumstances, Robbie was **holding up** very well. When she came to the part about not being allowed to visit Victor in the hospital, she could see that Robbie had trouble **fighting back the tears**. She gave him a few minutes to **pull himself together** before calling the other two children downstairs to tell them.

Just then, the front door opened and they heard a familiar voice, "I'm home! What's for dinner? The food in that hospital is horrible." The whole family **went crazy** when they saw him. Several minutes later after everyone had **calmed down**, Victor explained that he only had a slight concussion. The doctor wanted to keep him in the hospital overnight for observations, but he insisted on sleeping in his own bed. Victor was surprised that the doctor hadn't telephoned with the news. Looking embarrassed, Ramona went to the phone and put the receiver back on the hook.

yes   Ramona probably didn't want any interruptions when she had her conversation with Robbie.

_____   1. The children's bedroom probably was on the second floor.

_____   2. Robbie and his mother were probably eating dinner at the kitchen table as they talked.

_____   3. Victor probably only has one brother and no sisters.

_____   4. Victor's mother probably rushed over to the hospital after talking to Ramona.

_____   5. Ramona probably was going to call the other children to the kitchen to break the news to them too.

_____   6. The doctor probably forgot to phone Ramona.

_____   7. The doctor probably had tried to call Ramona to tell her that Victor had refused to follow her advice.

_____   8. Victor probably planned to return to work the following morning.

EXPANSION B

For each of the following stories, decide on the degree to which the person maintained self-control. Then finish the story.

Billy is seven years old. He went shopping in a large department store with his father, but somehow they got separated from each other. That was about ten minutes ago. Billy **kept a cool head** and went to a salesclerk.

How much control?   ✔ complete   _____ partial   _____ none

The clerk _made an announcement over the store's public address system_ .

1. Charles Berg spent the last few years writing a novel. When he finished, he sent it to a dozen publishing houses. Today, he got his twelfth rejection letter. Charles is beginning to **come apart at the seams**. He took all twelve letters, and he looked for a box of matches.

   How much control?   _____ complete   _____ partial   _____ none

   Then he _____ .

2. When Mrs. Skelley saw a dog bite her child while he was playing outside, she **went to pieces.** She ran out the door screaming and picked up her baby. Her screams were so loud they could be heard a block away.

   How much control?   _____ complete   _____ partial   _____ none

   A neighbor _____ .

3. Alice Suarez applied for a job that she really would like. Today, she received a letter in the mail informing her that someone else had been offered the position. Alice **fought back the tears**.

   How much control? _____ complete _____ partial _____ none

   Then Alice picked up the want ads and _____

   _____ .

4. Suzanne and Dan had planned to get married, but lately Suzanne has begun to have second thoughts. When she broke the wedding engagement with Dan, he **took the news rather calmly**. He told her that they probably shouldn't marry if she had serious doubts. Suzanne was relieved.

   How much control? _____ complete _____ partial _____ none

   She _____ .

5. The next day, Suzanne went to Dan's apartment to return the engagement ring to him. When he saw her take the ring from her finger, he **went crazy**. He ran into his bedroom, locked the door, and started breaking things.

   How much control? _____ complete _____ partial _____ none

   Suzanne _____ .

6. Last night, Mr. Juarez was nearly hit by a car when he was crossing the street on his way to the office. He was so upset at the time that he couldn't stop shaking for a few minutes, but he soon **pulled himself together**, and went to work.

   How much control? _____ complete _____ partial _____ none

   Mr. Juarez _____ .

7. Patti West got a notice from the Internal Revenue Service that she had overpaid her taxes last year. Enclosed in the letter was a check for $3,500. Patti **didn't** even **blink an eye**.

   How much control? _____ complete _____ partial _____ none

   She _____ .

8. When the mayor announced cuts in the police and fire departments at a press conference, the crowd got angry and began booing him. In spite of this reaction, the mayor stayed and finished his speech. At the end, he thanked the audience for listening to him. Under the circumstances, the mayor **held up** pretty well.

   How much control? _____ complete _____ partial _____ none

   The mayor _____ .

9. John was at work when he heard the news that a neighbor's house had just caught on fire, and that the houses on the rest of the block were in danger of burning because of high winds. It takes John an hour to drive home. He **was beside himself** because he knew there was very little he could do to help.

   How much control? _____ complete   _____ partial   _____ none

   John _____ .

10. Amy spent a half hour looking everywhere in her apartment for her favorite sweater. Just when she had about given up all hope of finding it, her roommate walked in with Amy's sweater. She had borrowed it without asking Amy. It took Amy ten minutes to **calm down**.

    How much control? _____ complete   _____ partial   _____ none

    Then, she turned to her roommate and said, _____

    _____ .

11. Betty knew that business hadn't been very good lately. An important meeting was scheduled for that afternoon, and there were rumors that the company might announce layoffs for some of the most recently hired workers. Betty started working for this company only six months ago. As she went to the meeting, she **braced herself** for bad news.

    How much control? _____ complete   _____ partial   _____ none

    At the meeting, her worst fears were realized, but she _____

    _____ .

12. When Mike got his grades, he saw that they were much worse than what he had expected. He had been placed on academic probation, which meant that he was ineligible to play on the school football team. Mike **fell apart** at this news because football was his first love.

    How much control? _____ complete   _____ partial   _____ none

    He _____ .

13. Matt bought an expensive sports car just yesterday after waiting almost six weeks to take delivery. He parked it on an incline and forgot to put on the emergency brake. The car rolled backward, crashing into another car. When Matt saw what had happened, he tried to **get a hold of himself**, but he couldn't. He just kept walking around saying, "What am I going to do? What am I going to do?"

    How much control? _____ complete   _____ partial   _____ none

    After fifteen minutes of this, his friends _____

    _____ .

EXPANSION C

Refer to the events in the Situation at the beginning of this unit to answer the following questions. Use idioms from this unit in your answers.

1. What do you suppose Dan might have said to Victor if Victor had asked him how Ramona sounded on the phone?

_____

_____

2. How do you suppose Ramona would describe her mother-in-law's reaction to the news that her son was in an accident?

_____

_____

3. How might Ramona describe her brother-in-law's reaction?

_____

_____

EXPANSION D

Use idioms from this unit to complete the following roleplay, which takes place at a dinner party. One of you is a stock broker, and one of you is a professional tennis player. Decide which role you will play, and read only the description for your role.

Stock Broker: You are having a good time at this party, in part because the famous tennis pro and you seem to be getting along well, and in part because you sold all of your holdings in a particular stock just in time. You have inside information that the first thing tomorrow morning the company, Piezo Inc., will file for bankruptcy.

Tennis Pro: You are in a terrific mood because the stock in which you have invested all of your fortune, Piezo Inc., is selling at an all-time high. You decide to ask the stock broker you've just met whether she/he is recommending this stock for purchase.

Read and discuss the following.

1. *Primal therapy* is a form of psychotherapy developed in the 1970s in which patients are encouraged to relive traumatic events. In so doing, they release emotional tensions (often by screaming and crying) and break down psychological defenses. Do you think we can understand ourselves better if we lose our composure?

2. The B-17 and B-24 bombers that were used by the United States Air Force during World War II came equipped with emergency bell systems. It is thought that the expression, *push the panic button* may have come from these emergency bell systems. In a distressing situation where your natural reaction might be to panic, someone might say, *Don't push the panic button.* Think of situations where it might be appropriate to use this expression.

3. Certain kinds of jobs require people to keep their composure especially when tension or stress is high. Can you think of examples?

4. Before telling very bad or shocking news to someone, you might say something like, "You'd better sit down" or "Maybe you should sit down before I tell you this." What is the purpose of sentences like these? What kinds of news might be considered very bad or shocking?

5. Choose one of the following quotations. Explain its meaning, or think of a situation that illustrates it.

> *Those who can command themselves, command others.*
>
> **William Hazlett**

> *The ability to keep a cool head in an emergency, maintain poise in the midst of excitement, and refuse to be stampeded are the true marks of leadership.*
>
> **R. Shannon**

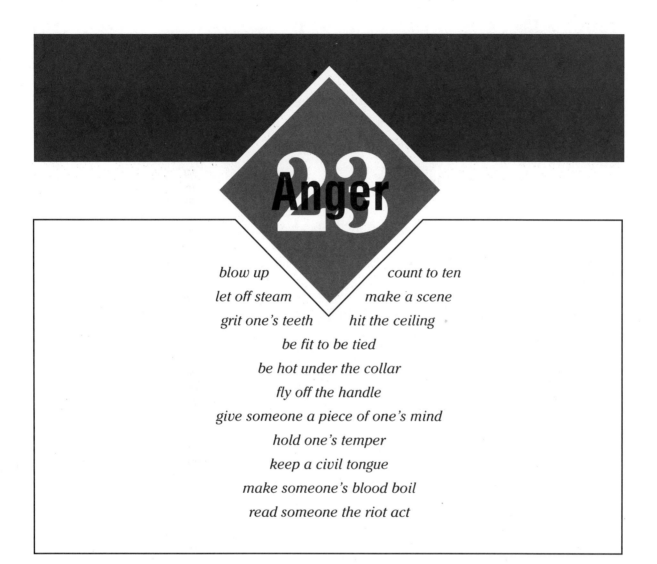

23 Anger

blow up   count to ten

let off steam   make a scene

grit one's teeth   hit the ceiling

be fit to be tied

be hot under the collar

fly off the handle

give someone a piece of one's mind

hold one's temper

keep a civil tongue

make someone's blood boil

read someone the riot act

WARM-UP

Anger is an emotional response to injury or injustice. Like all emotions, there are varying degrees of anger. A mild form of anger is irritation or annoyance. A strong form of anger is fury or rage. Keeping these definitions in mind, complete the following sentences.

I get irritated when _____ .

I get furious if _____ .

Do others know when you are irritated or angry? If so, how do you express your irritation or anger? If not, how do you hide it?

SITUATION

Read or listen to the following passage.

Sandy and Karen are students at Jones High School. Sandy is talking to Karen about a mutual friend she has just seen.

Sandy: Hey Karen, did you hear what happened to Ann?

Karen: No, what?

Sandy: Do you remember how worried she was about her history exam?

Karen: Yeah. It's tomorrow, I think. She said she probably would stay up all night studying for it.

Sandy: It's going to be hard for her to study if she doesn't have her notes, and she lent them to Ben Faber yesterday.

Karen: That's strange. I didn't think they knew each other very well. Anyway, what did he do? Lose them?

Sandy: You guessed it. I was over at Ann's when he called. He said he's looked everywhere, but just can't find them. Ann **is fit to be tied**.

Karen: I can't believe it. Murphy's Law: If something *can* go wrong, it will....

Sandy: And at the worst possible time. Anyway, on the phone, Ann was real nice to him and she told him not to worry about it. But as soon as they hung up, she **blew up**. I don't think I've ever seen her that angry before.

Karen: Can you blame her? What is she going to do? Without those notes, she'll never pass the exam. I'll tell you, I wouldn't want to be in her shoes.

Sandy: Or Ben's.

Karen: You can say that again.

ANALYSIS & EXPLANATION

Circle the best answer to the question below. Then turn to the appendix, where each answer is explained. If your choice is incorrect, choose again.

Why did Ann show her anger to her friend, Sandy, but not to Ben?

A. Ann probably was too surprised at first to feel any anger.

B. Ann probably feels she doesn't know Ben well enough to show her anger to him.

C. Ann probably didn't realize that Sandy saw her get angry.

ATTITUDE

Ann feels that there are times when she should try to hide or control her anger as well as times when she can release it or express it openly.

EXPANSION A

Read each passage below. Then respond to the true-or-false statements that follow it.

As it turns out, Ben didn't really lose Ann's notes. In fact, he lent them to his friend, Mike. Ben owed Mike a big favor, so he couldn't say no when Mike asked him if he could see Ann's notes. Ben thought if he told Ann the truth, she probably would have **hit the ceiling**. If someone had done the same thing to Ben, he probably wouldn't have reacted as calmly as Ann had. He probably would have **flown off the handle**. Ben never could **hold his temper**. In fact, he **blows up** a lot.

__T__ Ben kept the truth from Ann because he was afraid of what Ann might do.

_____ 1. Ben probably would have reacted in a similar way if Ann had lost his notes.

_____ 2. It doesn't take much for Ben to get angry.

_____ 3. Ben is usually very calm.

As soon as Ben finished talking to Ann, he tried to find Mike and get the notes back. He found Mike in the school parking lot. Just as Mike handed Ben the notes, Ann appeared. At first, she thought that Mike had found the notes, but then she overheard Mike thank Ben for lending them to him. First, she tried to control her anger by **gritting her teeth**, and then by **counting to ten**, but neither worked. She knew she wouldn't be able to **keep a civil tongue** this time. The situation really **made her blood boil** and Ann knew that this time she had to **let off some steam**. She went right up to Ben and started to **give him a piece of her mind**.

_____ 4. Ann hoped that her anger might lessen if she let some time pass.

_____ 5. Ann was so angry that she could almost feel her body temperature rise.

_____ 6. Ann knew she had to release some of her anger.

_____ 7. Ann gave Ben some words of wisdom.

ANGER ⟨173⟩

LET OFF STEAM

At first, Mike couldn't figure out why Ann **was** so **hot under the collar**, but the reason soon was clear. Ann called Ben everything from a liar to a cheat, and she didn't care who heard her. Pretty soon, all the noise attracted a small crowd of students. Ann really **made a scene.** The noise got so loud that Mr. Porter, the history teacher, heard it. When he found out what had happened, he **read the riot act to** all three of his students. When Mr. Porter was finished yelling, his students went straight home and started studying for the exam.

_____ 8. Mike didn't understand the cause of Ann's anger at first.

_____ 9. Ann's loud display of anger caught the attention of people nearby.

_____ 10. Mr. Porter was afraid that the argument might turn into a riot.

EXPANSION B

Write *A* for Anger if the person in each of the following situations got angry. If the person was able to control his/her anger, write *C* for Control.

_A_   Bill used a word processor to input ten pages of a research paper he was writing. A systems error occurred and Bill lost everything. He **was fit to be tied.**

_____ 1. Sue promised her boss she would finish an important report in time for an important meeting. Sue forgot. Her boss **blew up** at her.

_____ 2. Steve owed Mark some money that was long overdue. When Mark reminded Steve, Steve wrote out a check. The check bounced. Steve wrote out a second check and it bounced too! When Mark saw Steve, he **read him the riot act.**

_____ 3. Jill borrowed her mother's pearl necklace without asking her first. When Jill's mother noticed it was gone, she immediately called the police to report it stolen. When she found out what had really happened, she **hit the ceiling**.

_____ 4. Nancy overheard one of her co-workers telling someone else lies about her. What she heard **made her blood boil**.

_____ 5. At a press conference, Senator Busch was asked if the rumor was true that she used her political influence to get jobs for some of her relatives. Although the rumors were completely false, the senator managed to **hold her temper**.

_____ 6. Russ works as a server in a restaurant. After eating dinner, one of his customers sneaked out of the restaurant without paying. When Russ found out what had happened, he **flew off the handle**.

_____ 7. Dave's boss asked him to submit a five-year plan for the company. Even though Dave did a thorough job, his boss rejected all of Dave's recommendations. When Dave got home, he **let off some steam** to his wife.

_____ 8. Robert is a waiter at a fancy restaurant. He overheard a customer unfairly criticizing a good friend of his. Robert knew if he came to his friend's defense, he might not receive a tip, so instead he just stood there **gritting his teeth**.

_____ 9. This morning, Mary dropped off her car at the garage for an annual inspection. She told the mechanics that if they discovered any major problems, they should call her before doing any work on the car. No one called. When she returned to pick up the car later the same day, the mechanic handed her a bill for $700. Mary refused to pay, and the mechanic refused to release the car to her. The argument got louder and louder. Soon, all the other people in the garage stopped what they were doing to listen to the two of them argue. They sure **made a scene**.

_____ 10. Jack arrived ten minutes early for a ten o'clock appointment with his dentist. The receptionist told him that the dentist was running a little behind. A half an hour later, Jack's name still had not been called. Finally, at 11:30, the receptionist told Jack the dentist was ready to see him. The delay meant that Jack' schedule for the rest of the day would be off. Jack's dentist could tell that Jack **was hot under the collar**.

_____ 11. Sally was walking to her office building which is on a street where major construction is taking place. Seeing her coming down the street, one of the male construction workers yelled out, "Hey, babe! How about a date tonight?" She ignored this comment, but when she got to her office she telephoned the construction company and **gave them a piece of her mind**.

_____ 12. Tony arrived at the airport an hour before his flight, just as the ticketing agent told him he should. When he presented his confirmed-seat ticket at the check-in counter, he was told that there were no seats left on his flight. The airline had overbooked his flight. Tony **counted to ten**, hoping that he wouldn't be as angry when he finished counting. He then calmly asked what arrangements the airline had made to get him to his destination quickly.

_____ 13. The same person repeatedly dialed Nancy's telephone number by mistake. Even though this happened seven times in one evening, Nancy **kept a civil tongue** when talking to the caller.

EXPANSION C

Try to imagine how you would react if you were in each of the following situations. Begin each response with *I would* + idiom. *I'd probably say/do....* If you are working alone, write down your responses. If you are working with a classmate, say your responses aloud.

You return to your car after doing some shopping at the local mall. You notice a fresh dent in the car door. The same thing happened the last time you were at this mall.

_____ *I would hit the ceiling. I'd probably say, "Oh, hell. Not again."*

1. You emphasize to your server that the steak you ordered should be rare. When it comes, it is well done. You summon the server, who tells you that he/she distinctly remembers that you said you wanted your steak well done.

_____

2. You have been standing in the checkout line for fifteen minutes at the supermarket. A stranger cuts in line in front of you.

_____

3. Your best friend borrows your car for the day. The last time you drove the car, the tank was full. Your friend returns the car with the tank almost empty. You don't notice until it's too late. You run out of gas in the middle of a busy intersection.

_____

4. You studied hard for a test in one of your classes, but you didn't get a good grade. The test contained a lot of tricky questions. Your teacher asks you what you thought of the exam.

_____

5. You are taking a taxi to the airport to catch a flight. The driver gets lost along the way and you end up missing your flight. You decide not to tip the driver. The driver calls you a cheapskate.

_____

6. You have an appointment with someone who wants to do business with you. The person arrives twenty minutes late and makes no apology.

_____

7. You take your favorite coat to the local dry cleaners. After picking it up and returning home, you notice that there are several small holes in it. Needless to say, the holes are not supposed to be there. When you return with the coat and ask for some sort of compensation, the owner refuses.

_____

8. You receive a notice from the telephone company stating that service will be cut because you haven't paid your bill. You check your records and find that you did pay. In fact, you always pay your bills early and in full. You pick up the receiver to call the business office of the telephone company, but your line is dead.

_____

9. You give some money to your roommate to buy a gallon of milk. Later that day, you pour yourself a glass of milk and begin to drink it. It tastes sour. You notice that the expiration date stamped on the milk carton has passed. This is not the first time your roommate has done this.

_____

10. You spent most of the afternoon preparing lasagna for a dinner party you are hosting this evening. You put the casserole in the refrigerator and go upstairs. An hour later, you check on the food only to discover that a big piece has been cut from the dish! There's only one other person in the house—your 12-year-old son.

_____

> _I was angry with my friend:_
> _I told my wrath, my wrath did end._
> _I was angry with my foe:_
> _I told it not, my wrath did grow._
> **William Blake**

1. Work with a classmate to complete this roleplay, which takes place in an expensive restaurant after all of the customers have left. One of you is the manager, and one of you is the server. Decide which part you will play, and read only the paragraph that describes your role.

   Manager: A customer **read the riot act to** your best server after she/he spilled soup all over the customer's lap. The customer **made quite a scene**. You decide to ask the server what happened.

   Server: You dislike working as a server even though you are excellent at your job and you make very good money in tips. The incident with the customer really **made your blood boil**, so you tell your boss you have decided to quit.

2. Work with a classmate to complete this roleplay, which takes place one evening in front of a house located in an urban neighborhood. The characters are the owner of the house and the parent of a teenage son who lives on a nearby block. Decide which part you will play, and read only the paragraph that describes your role.

   Owner: You hear a noise outside, turn on the porch light, and see several teenagers running away. You recognize one of them. You go outside and notice a freshly painted message sprayed across your front door. You **hit the ceiling** and telephone the parents of the teenager you recognize.

   Parent: Your son just came home very upset. He says he was with some friends and one of them had a spray can of paint that he used on a house nearby. Your son claims he was an innocent bystander, and you believe him. However, he doesn't want to give you the name of the friend who is a graffiti artist. The telephone rings.

3. Work with a classmate to complete this roleplay between a shopper and a salesperson. Decide which role you will play, and read only the paragraph that describes your role.

   Shopper: At 8:00 this morning, you saw an ad in today's newspaper for a television set on sale at a local appliance store. You were the first customer in the store at 9:00. The salesperson tried to talk you into buying a more expensive set. When you insisted on buying the advertised set, the salesperson told you that the store had none in stock, and that it would take at least three weeks before the next shipment arrives. You **are fit to be tied**.

   Salesperson: A customer wants to buy a television set that was advertised in today's newspaper, but that set is out of stock. You try to interest the customer in a different set, which happens to be more expensive than the advertised one. You explain that delivery of the advertised item isn't expected for another three weeks. Your boss told you yesterday that if one more customer gets angry with you, you could lose your job. You do everything you can to please this customer.

> *Anger as soon fed is dead.*
> *'Tis starving makes it fat.*
>
> *Emily Dickinson*

1. The relationship you have with another person might determine whether or not you can **give that person a piece of your mind**. In your country, are you *more* likely or *less* likely to **blow up** at each of the following: a stranger; a friend; a family member; an acquaintance of equal status (such as a fellow student), one of lower status (such as someone you pay to do a service), or one of higher status (such as someone in a position of authority)?

2. The Roman philosopher Seneca said that "the greatest remedy for anger is delay." Which idiom illustrates this saying? What other techniques can be used to reduce anger?

3. Which of the idioms in this unit contain words that refer to heat or temperature? What is the relationship of heat and temperature to anger?

4. Some people think that it is better to release their anger rather than keep it inside for a long time. The idea is that anger added to anger will fill us up and one day we will explode. What do you think? Is it better to **let off steam** from time to time, or to keep it inside?

5. Choose one or more of the following sayings or quotations, or choose one that appeared earlier in the unit. Explain its meaning, or think of a situation that illustrates it.

> *Don't get mad, get even.*
>
>   *Robert Kennedy*

> *Swallowing angry words is much easier than having to eat them.*
>
>   *Anonymous*

> *People who fly into a rage always make a bad landing.*
>
>   *Will Rogers*

24 Personal Space

move over   elbow room

be underfoot   breathing space

elbow one's way   be in the/one's way

be packed in (like sardines)

breathe down someone's neck

get in the/one's way

get out of the/one's way

look over someone's shoulder

make room for someone

spread (one's things) out

stay out of one's way

WARM-UP

In his 1959 book *The Silent Language,* anthropologist Edward T. Hall proposed a model to describe how people in the United States often use *personal space* (the area around people that they control or use). Try to match the distance with the type of encounter.

Distance (inches)

_____ 1. Very Close (3"-6")
_____ 2. Close (8"-12")
_____ 3. Near (12"-20")
_____ 4. Neutral (20"-36")
_____ 5. Far Neutral (36"-60")
_____ 6. Public (60"-96")
_____ 7. Far Public (96"-240")
_____ 8. Great Distances (240"-?)

Types of Encounters:

a. used for social gatherings and business encounters
b. used by teachers and speakers at public gatherings
c. used in personal situations
d. used when comforting others or showing affection
e. used for many social situations when two people are meeting socially
f. used for social conversations, especially in groups
g. used for formal social interactions and business transactions
h. used for public speaking by public figures

Marie is a professional artist. An important client, Mrs. Edith Van Dame, commissioned Marie to do a painting of the church where she got married. She wants to give the painting to her husband for a wedding anniversary gift on Friday. It's now Tuesday evening. After a long day of painting, Marie is meeting a friend, Michael, at a coffeehouse.

Michael: What are you working on now?

Marie: The Van Dame piece. I know what you're going to say—

Michael: You haven't finished that yet?

Marie: That's what I thought you were going to say. No, I haven't finished yet. Will I? Not if everyone keeps bothering me.

Michael: What are you talking about?

Marie: I was at the church all day again today. Not five minutes after I had set up, I was surrounded by curiosity-seekers. They just stood there **looking over my shoulder**.

Michael: Maybe you should think of them as fans or admirers instead of the enemy.

Marie: I've tried. It doesn't work. You know how much I hate to have people **breathing down my neck**.

Michael: How about getting a boa constrictor or maybe a pitbull terrier?

Marie: Now there's a thought. If I'm going to finish before Friday, I might have to do something drastic.

Michael: Have you ever tried painting from a photo?

Marie: Actually, that's not a bad idea. Why didn't I think of that before?

ANALYSIS & EXPLANATION

Circle the best answer to the question below. Turn to the appendix, where each answer is explained. If your choice is incorrect, choose again.

Why has Marie been unable to finish the Van Dame painting?

A. The people who watch Marie paint distract her too much.
B. Marie can only paint when she feels inspired, and this painting doesn't inspire her.
C. Michael spends so much time with her that she can't finish.

ATTITUDE

Marie believes that there is an appropriate distance that should be observed between people, and that the distance depends upon the type of activity they are engaged in and the relationship of the individuals involved.

EXPANSION A

Read the passage below. Then respond to the true-or-false statements that follow it. Be prepared to defend your answers.

Rita is a reporter for *The Daily Post*, one of the largest newspapers in the country. A lot of changes in personnel have taken place recently in the newsroom, and Rita isn't happy with any of them. Rita is writing a letter to her former editor who is now stationed in the Middle East.

Dear Bill,

I'm on my lunch break, and I thought I'd write you a quick note to bring you up to date on what's been happening at the *Post*. In case you haven't heard yet: Carol Beesley's taken over your old job. The good news is that she's added two more reporters, but the bad news is that she put them in with me. You remember my tiny office, don't you? Now that there are three of us in there, I can't **spread out** anymore. In fact, just to get to my desk I have to **elbow my way** across the room. **We're packed in like sardines.** To try to **make room for the other two,**

I had to give up that little table that held my coffee maker. I don't need to tell you how much that coffee maker meant to me. I can barely function without it. I'll get more **elbow room** if it's the last thing I do.

On top of everything else, Carol always seems to be **getting in the way**. Every word I type, every phone call I make, there she is **looking over my shoulder**, offering suggestions and making corrections! She's always **breathing down my neck**. I guess she's just trying to be helpful, but I wish she would **get out of my way** and let me do my job. Yesterday was by far the worst. She **was underfoot** all morning. After a couple of hours of her suggestions, I got up and went down to the mail room. When I got back, she was actually sitting at my desk editing my work! I couldn't believe it, Bill. I walked right up to her and I asked her as sweetly as I could if I **was in her way**. I think I managed to embarrass her because she apologized and **moved over** real fast. Maybe now she'll **stay out of my way** and I'll have some **breathing space**. Gotta go. Deadlines to meet, you know. Miss you! Write soon.

_F_   Bill probably doesn't know who Carol is.

_____   1. Rita probably was happier when Bill was her editor.

_____   2. Bill probably requested a transfer to the Middle East to get away from Rita.

_____   3. Rita probably used to make coffee when she got to work in the morning.

_____   4. Carol probably doesn't spend much time in her own office.

_____   5. Rita probably has a secretary to type her news reports.

_____   6. Carol is probably just lonely.

_____   7. Bill and Rita probably know each other well.

EXPANSION B

Read each of the following situations. Then respond to the last statement in each situation; write *A* for Agree or *D* for Disagree.

A   John's dormitory room is small, and it is filled with his belongings. John has almost no **elbow room**. Maybe John should start thinking about moving to a bigger room or getting rid of some of his stuff.

_____ 1. Sam needed to get home early last night, and if he hadn't hurried he would have missed his train. Unfortunately for Sam, it was rush hour, and the streets were filled with people. Sam had to **elbow his way** through the crowd to get to the train station. Sam probably was able to catch his train.

_____ 2. Ken shares an office with Sue. They always seem to be **getting in each other's way.** Ken bumped into Sue three times this morning, and Sue tripped over Bill once. They probably should try to **stay out of each other's way.**

_____ 3. Jill volunteered to drive six of her friends to the beach. Her friends didn't know she had a sub-compact car. Jill really had to **pack them in like sardines** to get everyone in. The next time, Jill's friends will probably find another way to get to the beach.

_____ 4. When Bonnie sat down in the school library, she was the only one in the room, and she was able to **spread her books and papers out** all over the table. A half an hour later, every seat was taken. A student asked Bonnie if she wouldn't mind **moving over** a little so he could pull up an extra chair. Bonnie probably **made room for him**.

_____ 5. Andy was riding his bike when a dog stopped in the middle of the road in front of him. Andy yelled, "**Get out of the way**," but the dog apparently didn't understand English because it didn't move. Andy probably went around the dog.

_____ 6. Margaret was trying to cook dinner, but her husband kept **looking over her shoulder** to make suggestions. He only left the kitchen when Margaret told him he **was in her way**. Margaret probably was happy to have a little extra **breathing space.**

_____ 7. Tom's boss needed a report finished by the end of the day, and she kept coming in every ten minutes to see if Tom had finished it. Tom couldn't work well with his boss **breathing down his neck**. Tom probably finished the report on time.

_____ 8. Martha is always happy when her grandchildren come to visit, but she is always happy when they leave, too. That's because it doesn't take long before the kids **are underfoot**. When that happens, Martha probably can't get much housework done.

EXPANSION C

Refer to the events in the Situation at the beginning of this unit to complete the following activities. Use idioms from this unit in your responses.

1. Imagine that Marie and Michael are at the coffee house. They are at a table for four. Soon, the room gets very crowded, and their waiter asks them if they wouldn't mind **moving over** to **make room for** three more people. Write what might happen next.

2. Imagine that Marie has returned to the church the next day to finish the painting. In the spot where she normally works are two unlicensed street vendors who have **spread their goods out** all over the sidewalk. Write what might happen next.

> *Good fences make good neighbors.*
> *Robert Frost*

EXPANSION D   Use idioms from this unit to complete the following activities.

1. Work with a classmate to complete this roleplay, which takes place between two students in the kitchen of their apartment. Decide which role you will play, and read only the part that describes your role.

   Student A: You and your roommate are giving a dinner party. You normally do the cooking, but your roommate insisted on cooking this time. You are worried, so you stay close to the kitchen to make sure everything goes all right.

   Student B: You and your roommate are giving a dinner party. Your roommate usually does the cooking, but you think you're a better cook, so you are cooking this time. Your roommate is supposed to clean the apartment.

2. You just took a train from the city center to your home in the suburbs. Far more people were traveling than there were seats. Many people had to stand, and it was difficult to pass through the aisle. You decide to write a letter of complaint to customer service. What do you say?

1. For each of the following statements that express anger, who probably controls the space—the speaker or the listener? What do you base your answer on?

> Get out of my sight!
> Go away.
> If that's how you feel, I'm leaving.
> Leave me alone.

2. Drivers in the United States may become uneasy or angry when two moving vehicles get very close to each other. Driving too closely to the rear of another vehicle is known as *tailgating*. Some drivers send a message to tailgaters by putting the following sticker on the bumper of their vehicles:

> If you can read this, you are too close.

Positioning one vehicle too closely in front of another also can cause drivers to become uneasy or angry. When the driver of vehicle X passes vehicle Y but does not leave much space between the vehicles after passing, the driver of vehicle Y might say something like, "Did you see that? That guy just *cut right in front of me!*"

Driving very closely to another vehicle may be objectionable primarily because it is hazardous or dangerous, but drivers may also become angry because tailgating can be seen as an invasion of personal space. What do you think?

3. When two people are seated uncomfortably close to each other, one person might say something like the following to the other: "If you get any closer, you'll be sitting on my lap." Think of situations where it might be appropriate to say this. When might it be inappropriate to say this?

4. If two people are competing for control over the same space, one might say to the other something like the following, "This office isn't big enough for the two of us. One of us has got to go." Other words can be substituted for office—for example, room, apartment, house, building, school. What might someone be doing that would tempt you to use this expression?

5. Sometimes, it is not obvious that a particular space "belongs" to another person. Before people take a seat in a public area, they may ask one of the following questions to someone who is nearby:

> Is this seat taken?
> Is anyone sitting here?
> Are you saving this seat for anyone?

Identify several situations where these questions might be appropriate. Where would it be inappropriate to ask them?

6. The illustration below shows three benches in a public park. Ask several classmates to mark the spot where they might sit. Then ask them what factors they considered in making their choice.

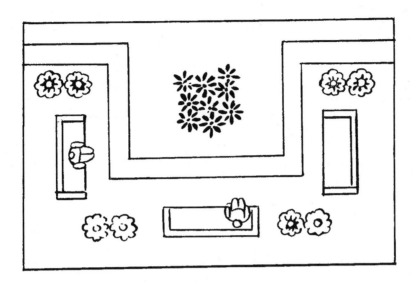

7. Explain the meaning of the quotation on p. 185, or think of a situation that illustrates it.

Appendix

Listed here are explanations of answer choice A for each unit's Analysis & Explanation section. For explanations of B and C, see the following pages.

A

Unit 1: Rob did get a B in the course, but he has no way of knowing if Tom is capable of getting the same good grade.

Unit 2: Emily and Karen wanted to buy a gift for Nurse Hallen. They didn't feel that they had to.

Unit 3: Ms. Thomas isn't required to greet the patients by name. She may not even be expected to do so.

Unit 4: Bello is enthusiastic about interviewing Fagan because of her reputation for working hard, but there is no indication that she is his first choice.

Unit 5: The children have several more hours before they have to go to bed.

Unit 6: The day that Greg begins college will be the day that he starts living a life that is independent of his parents. This is the best answer.

Unit 7: Lopez was upset to learn that one of his employees thought he was a terrible boss. However, there is something else that bothers Lopez about Goodrich—something about Goodrich's character.

Unit 8: Amy treated Paul unfairly in several ways. First, she ended the relationship suddenly and unexpectedly. Second, she said she was attracted to Paul because of his car. If true, then Amy took advantage of Paul. If not true, then Amy was being dishonest. This is the best answer.

Unit 9: On this particular day, both women went shopping together. However, there is nothing in the situation that indicates whether they prefer to shop alone or with someone else.

Unit 10: The test does worry Ben, but we don't know how likely he is to fail it without help from Sue. Sue has another reason for wanting to study with Ben.

Unit 11: Tom realized that his chances of succeeding were very slim. This is the best answer.

Unit 12: When she says that everyone has bad days, she implies that they are the exception and not the rule. This means that she thought Susan's behavior was not "normal."

Unit 13:   The decision to quit was perhaps easier to make because Jim didn't need the money, but this is not the primary reason.

Unit 14:   It is true that Antonio is very busy, especially with Giuseppe gone. It is also true that Francesca doesn't get to see much of her husband. However, she has a better reason for offering to help him at work.

Unit 15:   It would be understandable if John and Mark felt some resentment of Ed's success. However, nothing in the situation indicates that this is so.

Unit 16:   If Maude does say something to Peg, there is a chance that Peg will think that she doesn't like Timmy's visits. However, this is not at all the case.

Unit 17:   It is not because Dr. Rosenfield won a Pulitzer Prize that Bob wants to be in her class. It is her brilliant mind that impresses Bob.

Unit 18:   Felicia generally uses a babysitter when she needs someone to look after Tommy. These days, it seems that the candy striper program depends on Anita for far more support than does Felicia.

Unit 19:   The commission was asked to find solutions that were affordable and safe, but the mayor has other reasons for accepting the recommendations.

Unit 20:   She can't spell the winning word correctly, but that's not why she thinks George deserves to be recognized for his achievement.

Unit 21:   Pam was pleased about the brief amount of time it took the pharmacist to fill her order, but this is her first errand, and there is no information to indicate that she is running late.

Unit 22:   At first, Ramona appeared to be quite alarmed and upset.

Unit 23:   The news that Ben had lost Ann's notes caught her off guard, but it is incorrect to say she did not get angry. In fact, she was furious.

Unit 24:   The people who watch Marie work stand so close to her that she can't concentrate. This is the best answer.

B

Unit 1: Rob thinks that it is much too early for Tom to quit because there is still a good chance that he can pass the course. This is the best answer.

Unit 2: Emily and Karen don't know how much money Nurse Hallen makes. Emily thinks she is worth more than whatever it is that the hospital pays her.

Unit 3: Ms. Thomas prides herself on her ability to remember people's names. If she loses this ability, she will find it upsetting. This is the best answer.

Unit 4: Shuman recommends Fagan because she has a reputation for working diligently and efficiently. This is the best answer.

Unit 5: Mrs. Scheller hopes that she won't have any more interruptions. This isn't a bad answer, but there is a better one.

Unit 6: While it is true that a university education can be expensive, there is no information to indicate that finances are the reason for Steve's statement.

Unit 7: The telephone call that Lopez made might not have been personal and might have been made during his lunch break. The policy on the use of telephones will vary from company to company. We don't know what the policy is at Ajax.

Unit 8: Although Amy could have chosen a better place to break up with Paul, there is nothing in the dialog to suggest that Paul was upset because Amy ended the relationship at school.

Unit 9: Unlike Meg, Jill had no or very limited experience in using a VCR. Jill took advantage of Meg's experience to help her buy one. This is the best answer.

Unit 10: Ben said that he understood those chapters. We don't know how well Sue understood them.

Unit 11: After Tom made his decision about appealing to the judge, he went home and watched television. His decision to watch TV was independent of his decision about not voting.

Unit 12: Even though Nancy's behavior toward Susan was friendly, Susan was deliberately impolite to her again and again. This is the best answer.

Unit 13: Boredom is not the reason that Jim left his old job.

Unit 14: Antonio cannot run the restaurant properly by himself. He needs help. This is the best answer.

Unit 15: Unless changed, Ed's attitude may well result in the loss of more friends. This, however, is not John and Mark's major concern.

Unit 16: Harold thinks that this matter isn't serious enough to risk jeopardizing their relationship with Peg. This is the best answer.

Unit 17: It is because of Dr. Rosenfield's intellectual ability that Bob wishes he were in her class. She won the Pulitzer by applying her mind to a project. This is the correct answer.

Unit 18: Felicia usually hires someone to look after Tommy. She doesn't depend on Anita all the time to babysit.

Unit 19: The mayor was impressed with the work of the commission in identifying and explaining solutions to the city's trash problems. This is the best answer.

Unit 20: George was a poor speller in his childhood, but no more. There is nothing in the conversation to suggest that Mary's mother was surprised.

Unit 21: The pharmacist appeared to be friendly in a professional sort of way, but there is nothing in the passage to indicate that this was important to Pam.

Unit 22: Ramona was upset when she first heard the news, but after the initial shock, she was able to cope with the bad news. This is the best answer.

Unit 23: Karen points out that Ann and Ben don't know each other very well. Ann feels she can express her anger to people she knows very well, but she should control her anger in front of people she is just getting to know. This is the best answer.

Unit 24: Some artists can only work when they are in creative moods, but we don't know that Marie is like that.

C

Unit 1: We don't know what Rob's position is on dating.

Unit 2: Buying a gift for Nurse Hallen is Emily and Karen's way of thanking her for the kind treatment she gave them. This is the best answer.

Unit 3: Ms. Thomas probably did find it embarrassing that Mr. Wheatley greeted her by name, and she was unable to reciprocate. However, this is not the source of her concern.

Unit 4: Shuman was promoted from within the company, and he is recommending that another employee be promoted. However, no information is given to indicate that Bello would rather fill the position with someone from inside the company.

Unit 5: She was pleased to see that her sons were able to settle their disagreement through a compromise. This is the best answer.

Unit 6: When Greg goes off to college, Steve may well have to do chores that Greg has done, like mowing the lawn. However, this is not the reason for Steve's statement.

Unit 7: What is bothering Lopez is the realization that one of his employees deceived him and his wife. He is annoyed by Goodrich's dishonesty. This is the best answer.

Unit 8: We do not know for sure that Amy ended the relationship because she has a new boyfriend.

Unit 9: This shopping experience probably resulted in the two women becoming better acquainted, but this is not the reason they went shopping together.

Unit 10: Sue thinks that both of them will benefit by coming together and sharing information. This is the best answer.

Unit 11: Tom's candidate won the election, but no information was given to indicate that the candidate was expected to win.

Unit 12: On this morning, Susan did most of the talking. We have no information, however, about how much or how often Susan usually talks in the morning.

Unit 13: Jim was good at his old job, but it didn't bring him any happiness. He decided to pursue a career that he thought would bring happiness. This is the best answer.

Unit 14: The quality of service at the restaurant might suffer, but Francesca is more concerned about her husband than she is about the restaurant.

Unit 15: Ed's attitude has changed for the worse as a result of his successes on the basketball court. Ed's high opinion of himself irritates John and Mark. This is the best answer.

Unit 16: There is no indication that a conversation of this sort might take place when Timmy is around. In fact, they probably would make sure that Timmy wouldn't overhear them talking.

Unit 17: Bob may or may not be interested in health care issues. Even if he were interested, there is no information to suggest that these issues are included in the course syllabus.

Unit 18: Both the volunteers at the hospital and her daughter are depending on Anita to help them, but Anita feels she must support the hospital because she already has committed herself. This is the best answer.

Unit 19: The problem is one that needs to be solved soon or it will become worse, but the mayor has other reasons for accepting the recommendations.

Unit 20: George wasn't always good at spelling. His achievement today came about through great effort and in spite of obstacles and discouragement. This is the best answer.

Unit 21: Pam had only a half hour to get several errands done, so time was important to her. She was impressed by the speed at which the pharmacist worked. This is the best answer.

Unit 22: Ramona was able to function quite effectively.

Unit 23: Sandy was visiting Ann at the time of the telephone call, so it is highly unlikely that Ann did not realize she was there.

Unit 24: Marie works on the Van Dame painting during the day. She met Michael in the evening.

Glossary

a

add insult to injury   do damage twice to someone or to someone's feelings; do something that injures someone and then hurt that person's feelings, the total effect being excessive (Unit 8: Fairness)

at a snail's pace   extremely slowly (Unit 21: Speed)

b

bail out at the first sign of trouble   quit at the earliest opportunity; admit defeat when things begin to get difficult (Unit 1: Perseverance)

bare one's soul   be completely honest with someone, especially by revealing innermost thoughts and very personal feelings (Unit 7: Honesty and Directness)

be a babe in the woods   be lacking in experience and therefore easy to deceive or cheat (Unit 9: Experience)

be a big boy/girl now   be old enough to know better; be old or mature enough to be able to make one's own decisions (Unit 6: Independence)

be a dirty, rotten thing   be an unfair practice or action (Unit 8: Fairness)

be a hit below the belt   be an unfair action; do something that is outside of the rules; do something wrong or illegal (Unit 8: Fairness)

be a loner   be someone who prefers to work apart from others or to do things in isolation (Unit 10: Cooperation)

be a low blow   be an unfair action; do something that is outside of the rules of accepted behavior (Unit 8: Fairness)

be a long shot   be highly unlikely; have a very low probability of success (Unit 11: Improbability)

be a natural born something   someone who is suited by nature for a particular job or activity (Unit 3: Natural Ability)

be a whiz at something   be someone who has remarkable skill at doing something (Unit 3: Natural Ability)

be all or nothing   be an offer that is not open to negotiation; be the first and only offer (Unit 5: Compromise)

be all thumbs   be clumsy; act in an awkward way or manner (Unit 3: Natural Ability)

be an old hand at something   know how to do something because of much experience (Unit 9: Experience)

be an underhanded thing to do   act unfairly or unethically (Unit 8: Fairness)

be an uphill battle/struggle   be an effort in which success is difficult because of resistance or obstacles to it (Unit 11: Improbability)

be (as) sharp as a tack   be intellectually quick and accurate (Unit 17: Intellectual Competence)

be beside oneself   be in a state of extreme agitation (Unit 22: Composure)

be cool toward someone   be unfriendly to someone by being rudely brief in speech or abrupt in manner (Unit 12: Friendliness)

be down in the dumps   be unhappy; feel sad or depressed (Unit 13: Happiness)

be down to earth   be approachable; be free from pretensions, vanity, egotism (Unit 15: Humility)

be fit to be tied   be quite angry or very upset with someone or about something that happened (Unit 23: Anger)

be green   be inexperienced; lack familiarity with something, sometimes because of young age (Unit 9: Experience)

be hot under the collar   be angry or very upset with someone or about something that happened (Unit 23: Anger)

be in over one's head   be beyond one's ability to understand or deal with a situation (Unit 14: Limitations)

be in seventh heaven   be extremely happy or in an exceptionally good mood (Unit 13: Happiness)

be in the/one's way   be in one's path; placed so as to block the way (Unit 24: Personal Space)

be like looking for a needle in a haystack   be extremely unlikely or nearly impossible to find (Unit 11: Improbability)

be off base   be incorrect (Unit 19: Problem Solving)

be (off) on one's own   be independent; be self-supporting (Unit 6: Independence)

be old enough to look after oneself   be at an age where one need not depend on others (Unit 6: Independence)

be on cloud nine   be extremely happy or be in an exceptionally good mood (Unit 13: Happiness)

be on top of the world   be extremely happy or in an exceptionally good mood (Unit 13: Happiness)

be out in left field   be very much or completely wrong; misjudge something greatly; be completely unaware or ignorant of events (Unit 17: Intellectual Competence)

be out of one's hands   not be in a position to influence or change an outcome (Unit 11: Improbability)

be out to lunch   be inattentive; be absent mentally; be intellectually inactive (Unit 17: Intellectual Competence)

be packed in (like sardines)   be very close together; be uncomfortably close together; be so close that one cannot move (Unit 24: Personal Space)

be right on target   be correct; be on schedule (Unit 19: Problem Solving)

be stretched to the limit   be functioning at maximum capacity (Unit 14: Limitations)

be stuck up   be conceited; have an excessively favorable opinion of one's abilities, appearance, importance, etc. (Unit 15: Humility)

be the cream of the crop   be the best (Unit 20: Individual Achievement)

be the underdog   be the least likely person to succeed; be the least favored (Unit 11: Improbability)

be tickled pink   be very pleased or happy for someone or about something that happened (Unit 13: Happiness)

be too big for one's britches   feel more important than one really is (Unit 15: Humility)

be top dog   be the person with the highest authority or greatest prestige in a group; be the champion or the winner (Unit 20: Individual Achievement)

be two-faced   be deceitful by intentionally misleading someone; be dishonest by saying one thing to one person and the opposite to another (Unit 7: Honesty and Directness)

be underfoot   be in a position so as to form an obstruction (Unit 24: Personal Space)

be up front   be honest and straightforward in dealings with others (Unit 7: Honesty and Directness)

be wet behind the ears   lack experience or familiarity with something, sometimes because of young age (Unit 9: Experience)

beat around the bush   be evasive; avoid giving an answer or taking a position (Unit 19: Problem Solving)

beat the odds   succeed even though the chance of success is small (Unit 11: Improbability)

bend over backwards for someone   do whatever is necessary to help or please someone (Unit 2: Acts of Kindness)

bite off more than one can chew   commit oneself to doing more than one is capable of doing properly (Unit 14: Limitations)

blow up   become violently angry very quickly (Unit 23: Anger)

brace oneself   prepare oneself for distressing news (Unit 22: Composure)

breathe down someone's neck   follow someone closely, watching that person's movements carefully (Unit 24: Personal Space)

breathing space   enough space to permit ease of movement (Unit 24: Personal Space)

bring up the rear   be last in achieving something or in competing against others (Unit 20: Individual Achievement)

burn the candle at both ends   work to the point of exhaustion, often with a sacrifice in quality (Unit 14: Limitations)

burn the midnight oil   stay up late to work, usually on homework or other school assignments (Unit 4: Hard Work)

C

call it quits   admit defeat; stop doing something (Unit 1: Perseverance)

calm down   become quiet; regain composure (Unit 22: Composure)

can't do everything at once   refuse to take on any more work because one is already functioning at maximum capacity (Unit 14: Limitations)

cards are stacked against one   arrange things so that a person has an unfair advantage or disadvantage (Unit 11: Improbability)

come a long way   make a great deal of progress; achieve a lot, especially in the face of difficulties or obstacles (Unit 20: Individual Achievement)

come apart at the seams   become upset to the point where one risks losing self-control or composure (Unit 22: Composure)

come in first/second/third/last   be the best/second best/third best/ worst in a competition (Unit 20: Individual Achievement)

come to the rescue   help someone in need, especially in an emergency situation (Unit 2: Acts of Kindness)

count on someone   depend on someone; rely on someone for support or help (Unit 18: Dependability)

count someone out   exclude oneself or someone else from participating in an activity (Unit 18: Dependability)

count to ten   count from one to ten, usually aloud and slowly, in the hope that when the counting is finished, the anger will be gone or will be less; postpone action when angry (Unit 23: Anger)

cut the apron strings   leave a nurtured environment or support system; become emotionally independent from another (Unit 6: Independence)

d

do back-breaking work   do very difficult and demanding physical work; engage in an activity requiring great physical exertion (Unit 4: Hard Work)

do one's part   do the expected share of work (Unit 18: Dependability)

do someone a favor   do something out of kindness, rather than out of a sense of justice or for remuneration (Unit 2: Acts of Kindness)

drag one's feet   move slowly, sometimes with reluctance (Unit 21: Speed)

drop a course/class   withdraw from being a part of a course or class (Unit 1: Perseverance)

e

eat humble pie   be forced to admit mistakes or failures, especially in front of others and in a way that causes embarrassment (Unit 15: Humility)

elbow one's way   shove aside with one's elbow; make one's way by pushing or shoving with the elbow (Unit 24: Personal Space)

elbow room   enough room to move about or function in (Unit 24: Personal Space)

eyes are bigger than one's stomach   think one can eat more than one really can (Unit 14: Limitations)

f

fall apart   lose control of oneself (Unit 22: Composure)

fall down on the job   fail to work well; make a mistake while at work; not perform at a satisfactory level (Unit 4: Hard Work)

feather in one's cap   recognition for an accomplishment; prize or award for an achievement (Unit 20: Individual Achievement)

feel as if one is being pulled in a hundred/thousand/million different directions   feel overwhelmed by the demands that others are placing on one (Unit 14: Limitations)

feel blue   feel sad, discouraged, or mildly depressed (Unit 13: Happiness)

feel down   feel sad, discouraged, or mildly depressed (Unit 13: Happiness)

feel like a million bucks   be very happy or in an exceptionally good mood (Unit 13: Happiness)

fend for oneself   provide or earn a living for oneself (Unit 6: Independence)

fight back the tears   try to keep from crying (Unit 22: Composure)

find middle ground   agree on an intermediate position or solution between two opposites or extremes (Unit 5: Compromise)

flow with the tide   do what everyone else does for the sake of harmony; not object (Unit 16: Harmony)

fly off the handle   become angry very quickly and usually very loudly; release anger without thinking about consequences to oneself (Unit 23: Anger)

forgive and forget   stop feeling resentment toward a person and no longer take note of a complaint or incident (Unit 16: Harmony)

g

get a hold of oneself   get control of oneself; regain composure (Unit 22: Composure)

get a move on   begin doing something; start action on something (Unit 21: Speed)

get a raw deal   be treated unfairly (Unit 8: Fairness)

get ahead   be successful in business or society (Unit 20: Individual Achievement)

get along   live or work together in a friendly way (Unit 16: Harmony)

get down to brass tacks   identify and examine the most detailed parts of something; begin working on a problem in a serious manner (Unit 19: Problem Solving)

get in the/one's way   get in a position to obstruct or interfere (Unit 24: Personal Space)

get moving   start doing something (Unit 21: Speed)

get one's feet wet   become experienced; do something for the first time (Unit 9: Experience)

get/have one's own way   get what one wants without having to compromise (Unit 5: Compromise)

get out of doing something   manage to avoid doing something that was expected, succeed in not doing what was expected (Unit 18: Dependability)

get out of the/one's way   move; leave; stop interfering or obstructing (Unit 24: Personal Space)

get something off one's chest   say something that one has wanted to say for some time but was reluctant to (Unit 7: Honesty and Directness)

get the ball rolling   start something; begin action of something (Unit 21: Speed)

get the show on the road   get started; begin to do something (Unit 21: Speed)

get to the heart of something   identify and examine the most essential and crucial parts of something (Unit 19: Problem Solving)

get up on the wrong side of the bed   be irritable to everyone; be annoyed by everything that happens for no known reason (Unit 12: Friendliness)

give-and-take   practice of dealing with others through compromise or mutual concessions (Unit 5: Compromise)

give someone a fair chance   treat someone fairly (Unit 8: Fairness)

give someone a fair shake   provide someone with an equitable opportunity or treat someone fairly and honestly (Unit 8: Fairness)

give someone a hard/tough time   make life difficult or unpleasant for someone (Unit 12: Friendliness)

give someone a piece of one's mind   angrily tell someone exactly what one thinks (Unit 23: Anger)

give someone a warm welcome   greet someone in a sincere and gracious manner (Unit 12: Friendliness)

give someone the cold shoulder   treat someone in an unfriendly way by interacting minimally with that person or by ignoring that person (Unit 12: Friendliness)

give someone the shirt off one's back   do whatever is necessary to help someone (Unit 2: Acts of Kindness)

give up   stop trying; surrender (Unit 1: Perseverance)

go crazy   be unable to control oneself (Unit 22: Composure)

go halfway   agree to modify one's position so that an intermediate point is reached between two opposing positions (Unit 5: Compromise)

go it alone   work or be alone; do something in isolation (Unit 10: Cooperation)

go our/their separate ways   stop working or being with another person; do something in isolation (Unit 10: Cooperation)

go out of one's way for someone   help someone, especially when it is inconvenient to do so (Unit 2: Acts of Kindness)

go to bat for someone   give aid; help in times of trouble or need (Unit 2: Acts of Kindness)

go to one's head   have the effect of making pretensions to superior importance (Unit 15: Humility)

go to pieces   lose control of oneself (Unit 22: Composure)

goof off   avoid doing work; waste time (Unit 4: Hard Work)

grit one's teeth   suppress one's anger, often because showing it would be counterproductive (Unit 23: Anger)

h

hands are full   be completely occupied; be functioning at maximum capacity; be unable to do additional work (Unit 14: Limitations)

hands are/were tied   be prevented from doing something; be unable to intervene (Unit 11: Improbability)

hang in there   keep doing something or continue with a project and not lose hope or courage (Unit 1: Perseverance)

have a bone to pick with someone   have a reason to complain or dispute (Unit 16: Harmony)

have a good head on one's shoulders   be intelligent or smart (Unit 17: Intellectual Competence)

have a green thumb   be skilled at growing plants (Unit 3: Natural Ability)

have a knack for something   have a special talent or aptitude for doing something (Unit 3: Natural Ability)

have a lot on the ball   be smart or clever (Unit 17: Intellectual Competence)

have a mind of one's own   do what one thinks best in spite of popular opinion; arrive at opinions independently (Unit 6: Independence)

have a nose for something   have an instinctual knowledge of something; have the ability or sense to discover something as if by smell (Unit 3: Natural Ability)

have a screw loose   think or reason in an illogical or irrational way (Unit 17: Intellectual Competence)

have a snowball's chance in hell   having virtually no chance of success (Unit 11: Improbability)

have a swollen head   have a higher opinion of oneself than is deserved; be vain, egotistical, and pretentious (Unit 15: Humility)

have an (good) eye for something   have an ability to make intellectual or aesthetic judgments (Unit 3: Natural Ability)

have been around   be very familiar with something (Unit 9: Experience)

have more work than one can handle   be overwhelmed with work (Unit 14: Limitations)

have the golden touch   have the ability to make large sums of money consistently (Unit 3: Natural Ability)

have two left feet   be clumsy; trip or fall down frequently (Unit 3: Natural Ability)

help (someone) out   give assistance to someone; provide help (Unit 2: Acts of Kindness)

hem and haw   avoid giving an answer to a problem or taking a position on an issue (Unit 19: Problem Solving)

hit the books   study; read homework assignments (Unit 4: Hard Work)

hit the bull's eye   identify or solve a problem exactly; be completely correct (Unit 19: Problem Solving)

hit the ceiling   become very angry (Unit 23: Anger)

hit the nail on the head   identify or solve a problem exactly; be completely correct (Unit 19: Problem Solving)

hold one's temper   restrain one's anger; keep anger inside of oneself, hiding it from others (Unit 23: Anger)

hold up   keep control of oneself; keep one's composure (Unit 22: Composure)

hold up one's end of the bargain   do one's share of work (Unit 18: Dependability)

hook up with someone   join or become associated with (Unit 10: Cooperation)

i

in a flash   extremely fast; quickly (Unit 21: Speed)

in no time (flat)   extremely fast; quickly (Unit 21: Speed)

j

join forces   come together for a shared purpose, usually for mutual benefit (Unit 10: Cooperation)

k

keep a civil tongue   speak in a courteous and respectful way even though one is angry or upset (Unit 23: Anger)

keep a cool head   stay calm and composed, especially in the face of adversity (Unit 22: Composure)

keep at it until one gets it right   continue to do something until it is completely acceptable or absolutely correct (Unit 1: Perseverance)

keep one's nose to the grindstone   work without interruption; continue to work without stopping (Unit 4: Hard Work)

know one's way around   be familiar or well-acquainted with something (Unit 9: Experience)

know something like the back of one's hand   know something extremely well; be thoroughly familiar with something (Unit 9: Experience)

know the ropes   have a thorough knowledge of something; be completely familiar with something through experience (Unit 9: Experience)

l

lay one's cards on the table   let someone know what one is going to do; show one's strengths and weaknesses to another; tell someone everything (Unit 7: Honesty and Directness)

leave someone high and dry   break a commitment to someone, usually resulting in great inconvenience to that person (Unit 18: Dependability)

leave the nest   move away from parent's home (Unit 6: Independence)

lend someone a (helping) hand   help someone; provide assistance to someone (Unit 2: Acts of Kindness)

let bygones be bygones   decide to forget past disagreements and become reconciled (Unit 16: Harmony)

let off steam   release anger, often by yelling or screaming (Unit 23: Anger)

let sleeping dogs lie   not provoke to anger or cause trouble if it can be avoided (Unit 16: Harmony)

let someone down   cause someone to be disappointed by not doing what was expected (Unit 18: Dependability)

like a bat out of hell   at top speed; extremely fast, often from fear or panic (Unit 21: Speed)

long face   an unhappy or gloomy expression on one's face (Unit 13: Happiness)

look like one lost one's best friend   appear to be extremely sad, dismal, or dejected (Unit 13: Happiness)

look over someone's shoulder   follow someone closely, watching that person's movements carefully (Unit 24: Personal Space)

look someone in the eye   face something or someone directly, bravely, and without shame (Unit 7: Honesty and Directness)

lose one's touch   lose one's ability to do something effectively (Unit 3: Natural Ability)

m

make a federal case out of something   exaggerate the importance of a complaint that is trivial (Unit 16: Harmony)

make a scene   bring attention to oneself through loud and angry behavior (Unit 23: Anger)

make it big   be very successful in life, usually implying fame and/or wealth (Unit 20: Individual Achievement)

make it on one's own   attain success without assistance from others (Unit 6: Independence)

make it to the top   become successful, victorious, or dominant (Unit 20: Individual Achievement)

make room for someone   give up space to another (Unit 24: Personal Space)

make someone feel at home   help someone feel at ease or comfortable (Unit 12: Friendliness)

make someone's blood boil   do something that causes someone to become extremely angry (Unit 23: Anger)

make something out of oneself   become a success or achieve one's goals (Unit 20: Individual Achievement)

make tracks   hurry up; go quickly (Unit 21: Speed)

make waves   create a disturbance, disagree or object, cause trouble by questioning what is accepted or done by others (Unit 16: Harmony)

meet someone halfway   settle differences by making concessions at an intermediate point between the opposing sides (Unit 5: Compromise)

middle-of-the-road   intermediate point between two extreme positions; neutral position
(Unit 5: Compromise)

miss the mark   be incorrect (Unit 19: Problem Solving)

move over   change position; move from one place to another (Unit 24: Personal Space)

n

not be born yesterday   be difficult to fool or deceive because of much experience (Unit 9: Experience)

not blink an eye   not show surprise; show no reaction; stay calm and composed (Unit 22: Composure)

not give an inch   refuse to compromise; keep original position (Unit 5: Compromise)

not give someone the time of day   be rude to someone by ignoring that person completely; treat someone
as having little importance; snub someone (Unit 12: Friendliness)

not have anything between one's ears   lack ordinary quickness and keenness of mind; be stupid
(Unit 17: Intellectual Competence)

not hold a candle to someone   compare unfavorably against another; be in an inferior or lesser class
(Unit 20: Individual Achievement)

not know enough to come in out of the rain   show no sound, practical judgment (Unit 17: Intellectual
Competence)

not know whether one is coming or going   be confused mentally; lack judgment (Unit 17: Intellectual
Competence)

o

offer one's services   help someone; volunteer one's time (Unit 2: Acts of Kindness)

open a can of worms   raise a complex problem or complicated situation that is likely to result in
disagreement (Unit 16: Harmony)

outdo oneself   surpass or exceed one's previous performance (Unit 20: Individual Achievement)

p

pass the buck   refuse to accept responsibility for an action or consequence, shift blame for an action onto
another person (Unit 18: Dependability)

pick someone's brain   ask someone a lot of questions (Unit 17: Intellectual Competence)

pitch in   contribute to a common cause; join in with others in getting something done
(Unit 10: Cooperation)

place first/second/third   finish in first/second/third place in a competition (Unit 20: Individual
Achievement)

play dirty   treat others unfairly or unethically (Unit 8: Fairness)

play fair   treat others fairly (Unit 8: Fairness)

play second fiddle to someone   take a smaller or less important role and consequently be noticed less
(Unit 20: Individual Achievement)

play with half a deck   act irrationally or foolishly; be stupid (Unit 17: Intellectual Competence)

pool one's resources   combine one's strengths with another for a common purpose (Unit 10: Cooperation)

pull one's own weight   do the work that others expect, do one's full share of work (Unit 18: Dependability)

pull oneself together   get control of oneself; regain composure (Unit 22: Composure)

pull the wool over someone's eyes   deceive someone; fool someone; trick someone (Unit 7: Honesty and
Directness)

put on airs   assume a self-importance in social situations that is undeserved, usually done by a pretentious
or egotistical person (Unit 15: Humility)

put on one's thinking cap   get into a state of mind that is marked by reflection or concentration
(Unit 17: Intellectual Competence)

put someone at ease   do things to help another person feel more comfortable or less nervous
(Unit 12: Friendliness)

put someone in someone's place   lower someone's self-esteem, especially an arrogant person (Unit 15: Humility)

put your/our/their heads together   collaborate with another/others on a task that requires thinking or mental activity (Unit 10: Cooperation)

r

read someone the riot act   give someone a strong warning; scold someone (Unit 23: Anger)

rock the boat   cause a disturbance that may spoil a plan (Unit 16: Harmony)

run oneself ragged   become exhausted from too much work or activity, especially over an extended period of time (Unit 14: Limitations)

s

save the day   succeed in helping someone who is in danger or trouble (Unit 2: Acts of Kindness)

see eye to eye   agree completely with someone, hold the same views or opinions of another person (Unit 16: Harmony)

see the writing on the wall   recognize that a particular event will happen; feel sure that something will happen in the future because something in the present indicates that it will (Unit 11: Improbability)

set a world record   do something more quickly than anyone else (Unit 21: Speed)

shoulder the responsibility   accept full responsibility (Unit 18: Dependability)

show off   try to get the attention of others by displaying one's abilities or accomplishments in a prominent way (Unit 15: Humility)

skirt the issue   be evasive; avoid taking a position or giving an answer (Unit 19: Problem Solving)

speak one's mind   say what one is thinking even if it upsets others or is critical of them (Unit 7: Honesty and Directness)

spread (one's things) out   distribute or place (one's things) over a wide area (Unit 24: Personal Space)

spread oneself too thin   be involved in so many projects that one risks not doing any of them well (Unit 14: Limitations)

stand on one's own two feet   achieve something without assistance from others (Unit 6: Independence)

stay out of one's way   stop interfering and remain that way; keep away (Unit 24: Personal Space)

step on it   go faster; hurry up (Unit 21: Speed)

stick to one's guns   refuse to change one's mind or alter one's position, usually out of principle (Unit 5: Compromise)

stick with it (to the bitter end)   continue to do something unpleasant until it is finished (Unit 1: Perseverance)

strike a happy medium   compromise to a point where everyone can agree (Unit 5: Compromise)

strike off on one's own   act independent of a group; work in isolation (Unit 10: Cooperation)

swallow one's pride   admit to a failure or mistake publicly, usually bringing some embarrassment to the person who is making the admission (Unit 15: Humility)

sweat it out   wait or continue anxiously until the end (Unit 1: Perseverance)

t

take care of oneself   be able to make decisions without approval or assistance from others (Unit 6: Independence)

take it easy   go or act slowly, slow down (Unit 14: Limitations)

take one's (good old) time   do something slowly without pressure (Unit 21: Speed)

take someone down a notch/peg or two   do something to make someone feel less important or significant, usually done to someone who is pretentious or egotistical (Unit 15: Humility)

take the bull by the horns   take direct action even though risks or dangers are present (Unit 19: Problem Solving)

take the news pretty well/badly   react to events well/poorly (Unit 22: Composure)

talk behind someone's back   gossip about someone without that person's knowledge (Unit 7: Honesty and Directness)

talk out of both sides of one's mouth   be dishonest by saying one thing to one person and something conflicting to another, or by giving conflicting information to the same person at different times; be hypocritical (Unit 7: Honesty and Directness)

team up with someone   join with someone else for a common purpose, often to work on a project (Unit 10: Cooperation)

tell it like it is   speak in a sincere, straightforward, and direct way (Unit 7: Honesty and Directness)

throw in the towel   quit; admit defeat; surrender (Unit 1: Perseverance)

toot one's own horn   make others aware of one's own accomplishments; say positive things about oneself; congratulate oneself publicly on one's achievements (Unit 15: Humility)

tough it out   endure or resist hardship (Unit 1: Perseverance)

turn one's back on someone   refuse to help (Unit 18: Dependability)

u

upset the applecart   do or change something with the result that others may be upset (Unit 16: Harmony)

w

walk on air   feel extremely happy, usually after receiving some particularly good news (Unit 13: Happiness)

warm up to someone   become more intimate and attached to someone (Unit 12: Friendliness)

welcome someone with open arms   address or welcome someone in a sincere and friendly way (Unit 12: Friendliness)

work like a dog   work hard, often for long hours (Unit 4: Hard Work)

work one's fingers to the bone   work hard, usually in manual labor (Unit 4: Hard Work)

worm out of something   avoid doing something that one previously agreed to do, often in spite of pressure to do it (Unit 18: Dependability)

z

zero in on something   find or identify something that one is looking for (Unit 19: Problem Solving)

Attitudes
Through Idioms

THOMAS W. ADAMS
AND SUSAN R. KUDER

SECOND EDITION

The revised edition of a classic Newbury House text, *Attitudes Through Idioms* presents idioms in groups relating to cultural ideas such as humility, compromise, anger, problem solving, and natural ability. The text's goal is to help students to understand the cultural context in which the idioms are used.

LEVEL: Intermediate

FEATURES:

▶ **Conceptually related idioms are presented together,** allowing learners to distinguish nuances in meaning and appropriateness.

▶ **Covers 270 idioms**

▶ **Target idioms are presented contextually** in dialogues, readings, exercises, and communication activities.

▶ **New to the Second Edition:** More authentic language, greater contextualization, and more interactive activities.

TEXT: 0-8384-3975-6
ANSWER KEY: 0-8384-4251-X
CASSETTE TAPE: 0-8384-5358-9
COMPACT DISC: 0-8384-5406-2

HEINLE & HEINLE PUBLISHERS
A Division of Wadsworth, Inc.
Boston, Massachusetts 02116 U.S.A.

ISBN 0-8384-3975-6

9 780838 439753

90000>

NORTHSTAR

Focus on Reading and Writing

Judy L. Miller
Robert F. Cohen

Advanced

 LONGMAN